Assessing the Generic Outcomes of College

Selections from Assessment Measures

Edited by Gary R. Pike

Assessment
UPdate
COLLECTIONS

Published by Jossey-Bass
A Wiley Imprint
989 Market Street, San Francisco, CA 94103-1741   www.josseybass.com

Jossey-Bass books and products are available through most bookstores. To contact Jossey-Bass
directly call our Customer Care Department within the U.S. at 800-956-7739, outside the
U.S. at 317-572-3986, or fax 317-572-4002.

Jossey-Bass also publishes its books in a variety of electronic formats. Some content that
appears in print may not be available in electronic books.

Library of Congress Cataloging-in-Publication Data available upon request

FIRST EDITION
PB Printing   10 9 8 7 6 5 4 3 2 1

Contents

Critical Thinking Assessment

Value-Added Assessment

Assessing the Generic Outcomes of College: Selections from "Assessment Measures"

The broad outcomes of a college education have been described using a variety of terms, including general education outcomes and generic skills or outcomes. I am particularly fond of Baird's (1988) characterization of these outcomes as the "diverse and subtle arts." Although the outcomes have gone by many names, higher education leaders and policy makers have consistently stressed the importance of the generic outcomes of college. Both the National Education Goals Panel (1991) and the Secretary of Education's (Spellings) Commission on the Future of Higher Education (U.S. Department of Education, 2006), for example, stressed the importance of assessing and improving the generic skills of critical thinking, communicating, and problem-solving. Given this high level of interest, it is not surprising that a significant number of "Assessment Measures" columns have focused on issues related to the assessment of the generic outcomes of a college education. Many of these columns are included in this collection, and they can be grouped into four broad categories: (1) commercially available measures of general education outcomes, (2) writing assessment, (3) assessment of critical thinking, and (4) assessing the value added by a college education. The first three categories roughly correspond to the content areas identified in major national reports, and the final category includes columns focusing on how best to represent the unique contributions of a college education.

Because the columns in this collection cover a span of almost 20 years, they provide an insight into the evolution in thinking about assessing the general outcome of college. It is also true, as the French writer Alphonse Karr noted, that the more things change, the more they remain the same. Thus, while the assessment of the generic outcomes of college has evolved over time, the same vexing issues plague assessment efforts. The twin themes of evolution and recurrence can be found in the columns comprised by this collection.

Commercially Available Measures

Institutions interested in assessing general education outcomes in the early 1980s were faced with a serious challenge—direct measures of these outcomes did not exist. As a result, colleges and universities turned to tests that were developed for other purposes, such as the ACT Assessment, Scholastic Aptitude Test (SAT), and the Graduate Record Examination (GRE). As I noted in the very first "Assessment Measures" column, the ACT, SAT, and GRE exams may have provided accurate and appropriate information about students' readiness for college or graduate school, but there were serious concerns about the appropriateness of using these exams to assess education programs.

The development of the College Outcome Measures Program (COMP) examinations in the mid- to late-1980s, followed by the introduction of the Academic Profile and the Collegiate Assessment of Academic Proficiency (CAAP), represented the first evolutionary wave in general education tests. These tests were developed specifically to assess general education outcomes. Both the COMP Comprehensive Examination and the shorter Objective Test were designed to be measures of effective adult functioning. One feature that made the COMP exams very popular for assessing general education outcomes was the ability to estimate score gains (that is, value added) over the course of a college education. Although the tests' developers provided recommendations about how results could be used to improve general education programs (see Forrest & Steele, 1982), the linkages between COMP scores and institutions' general education curricula were not direct. The Academic Profile and the CAAP exams represented a sort of mini-evolution within the first wave of general education assessments. Rather than focusing broadly on effective adult functioning, both the Academic Profile and the CAAP included content areas related to general education course-work (for example, English, social science, and the arts and humanities) and abilities that were thought to be enhanced by general education (writing, critical thinking, and quantitative skills).

Although the scores provided by the Academic Profile and CAAP exams had a closer correspondence to general education curricula, questions about the sensitivity of the tests remained. In fact, concerns about the sensitivity of the Academic Profile and CAAP were at the center of the negative report by Washington State's Joint Task Force. The report concluded that the Academic Profile, CAAP, and COMP exams were not appropriate for assessing general education outcomes at public institutions in Washington. In a later column on the criteria that should be used to evaluate assessment instruments, I too made a test's sensitivity to the effects of education programs an important criterion for judging the appropriateness of assessment instruments.

The introduction of the College Basic Academic Subjects Examination (College BASE) represented a second wave in the evolution of measures of general education outcomes. Unlike the Academic Profile, CAAP, and COMP exams, which measured student and institutional performance against the performance of other students/institutions (that is, norm-referenced tests), College BASE was designed to be a criterion-referenced test in which student and institutional performance were evaluated using predetermined standards. Revisions to the Academic Profile (the Academic Profile II) still made use of criterion-referenced evaluation, although norms were also provided. Criterion-referenced measures, such as College BASE, appeared to show greater sensitivity to educational effects. However, scores on these exams were still strongly influenced by students' entering ability levels and institutional selectivity. As a result, what students brought to college remained a more important factor in test performance than students' experiences during college (Pike, 1992).

The Collegiate Learning Assessment (CLA) represents the third wave of commercially available general education measures. Interestingly, this wave of general education assessment harks back to the

COMP Composite Examination. Like the Composite Examination, the CLA is a production, rather than a recognition, measure. That is, students must produce a response to a question or problem, rather than simply recognizing a correct answer. The CLA also provides an overall institutional score that does not link directly to the content of a general education curriculum. Here again, the test developers have suggested ways in which CLA scores can be used to make improvements in general education, and the CLA provides a measure of the value added by a college education. Despite improvements in the psychometric properties of the CLA brought about by nearly 20 years of research and experience with general education assessment, questions remain about the sensitivity of CLA scores to educational experiences (McCollum, 2010).

Writing Assessment

Several commercially available tests, such as CAAP and College BASE, contain multiple-choice assessments of college writing and also have optional test modules that include direct assessments of writing. Despite the availability of these writing assessments, and the writing assessment provided by the CLA, some institutions have decided to develop their own direct assessments of students' writing abilities. The two "Assessment Measures" columns about writing included in this collection identify several factors that should be taken into account in designing a writing assessment.

The first column identifies three basic questions that should be answered before implementing a writing assessment: What type of writing task should be used? What type of writing should be assessed? What type of scoring rubric should be used? The answers to these questions will significantly influence the form and structure of a writing assessment. An underlying assumption of this column is that institutions will select the type of writing assessment that most closely corresponds to the writing skills expected of students. For example, if an institution emphasizes learning to identify a question, research a topic, and write and revise a paper, a process writing approach to assessment would be most appropriate. Likewise, if students are expected to write persuasive papers, then persuasive prompts would be most appropriate. The goal should be a writing assessment that matches the writing curriculum of the institution.

The second column examines practical issues related to implementing a writing assessment. These practical considerations influence the accurateness and appropriateness (that is, reliability and validity) of the data produced by a writing assessment. Many of the techniques discussed in the column—use of anchor papers, training of raters, and testing to control for decay and drift—are essential to assure high levels of inter-rater agreement. Careful selection of anchor papers to represent specific levels of writing proficiency is also essential to ensure that judgments about student writing are appropriate.

Assessing Critical Thinking

The assessment of critical thinking faces many of the same issues as general education assessment and writing assessment. The first column in this category examines basic issues related to the assessment of critical thinking. Like writing assessment, the assessment of critical thinking requires that several fundamental questions be asked and answered: What is meant by critical thinking? Is critical thinking unidimensional or multidimensional? Is critical thinking a continuum or is it a series of stages? Again, the answers to these questions can guide an institution in selecting critical thinking assessments and help ensure that the data provide useful information for evaluating an institution's education programs.

Like commercially available tests of general education outcomes, measures of critical thinking have tended to come in waves. The first wave is represented by the Watson-Glaser Critical Thinking Appraisal (CTA) and the California Critical Thinking Skills Test (CCTST) in this collection. Both are relatively simple recognition measures that assume the development of critical thinking occurs along a single continuum. Both measures have been found to produce highly reliable (internally consistent) scores, but questions remain about their sensitivity to educational effects. The Tasks in Critical Thinking represents a modest departure from the CTA and CCTST. The Tasks in Critical Thinking is a production measure in which students construct a response to a question or problem.

Like the CTA and CCTST, the Tasks measure presumes that the development of critical thinking occurs along a single continuum.

The Reflective Judgment Interview is typical of the second wave of critical thinking assessments. The RJI requires that students construct a response to a realistic problem/dilemma, explain the rationale for the response, and evaluate the rationale. The paradigm underlying the RJI is a stage model in which students move from relatively simple stages of dualistic (that is, right versus wrong) reasoning, frequently based on authority, to much more complex stages in which multiple perspectives are taken into account. As with writing assessment, careful training and calibration of raters can yield high levels of inter-rater agreement. In addition, RJI scores increase with levels of educational attainment. Nevertheless, questions remain about the sensitivity of the RJI to specific educational programs or interventions.

The third wave in the assessment of critical thinking abilities is a measure developed by the National Center for Research on Evaluation, Standards, and Student Testing (CRESST). The CRESST measure represents the most radical departure from other critical thinking tests. The developers of the instrument did not view critical thinking as a generic skill. Instead they began with the premise that critical thinking is domain-specific and requires knowledge of a discipline or content area. Simply put, critical thinking in biology is not the same as critical thinking in business, because each domain requires very specific content knowledge. The CRESST measure also differs from other critical-thinking measures in that it assesses content knowledge, problem-solving ability, and motivation. Although assessment of critical thinking using the CRESST approach can be complex and time-consuming, issues of insensitivity to educational effects are less pronounced, due perhaps to the focus on discipline-specific knowledge.

Assessing Value Added

It should be clear by now that I believe the sensitivity of assessment instruments to the effects of educational programs is critically important. Assessment instruments that are sensitive to educational effects can provide accurate and appropriate information about the effectiveness of education programs for accountability to external stakeholders and for institutional improvement. Measures that are not sensitive to educational effects, either because they measure a stable trait or because scores are confounded by the entering ability levels of students, can produce extremely inaccurate and inappropriate results.

One approach that has been used to highlight the unique contributions of a college education is the use of value-added analysis. The concept of value added comes from economics and originally referred to the increase in the value of a product as it moves through each stage of the manufacturing process from raw material to finished product. In the 1980s, the College Outcome Measure Program was quick to adopt the value-added metaphor. Test developers used mean differences between a cohort of students' freshmen and senior scores on the exams as an indication of the gains in general education outcomes (that is, value added) produced by the institution. Because many institutions were not willing or able to administer a test, wait at least four years, and administer the test again, estimated gain scores (based on students' ACT scores at entry) were developed for the COMP exam. The state of Tennessee used these mean gain (or difference) scores to award a portion of performance-funding dollars to institutions.

In the late 1980s and early 1990s, researchers at the University of Tennessee, Knoxville (UTK) undertook a longitudinal study to evaluate the use of gain scores in the performance funding model. Based on their analysis they concluded that gain scores did not provide either accurate or appropriate measures of the quality and effectiveness of education programs at UTK. An earlier study had raised serious questions about the use of estimated gains scores in assessment (Banta et al., 1987). This column generated considerable debate between the developers of the COMP exam and UTK researchers in the same issue of *Assessment Update* (Volume 4, Number 2).

Research on methods of measuring change during college continued at UTK, and in a subsequent column I outlined a variety of measures that could be used to evaluate the effects of college on student learning and development. That column, which is included in this collection, examined the pros and cons of approaches ranging in complexity from relatively simple gains scores and estimated gains scores to more complex measures, such as residual gain scores, mixed-effect models, and growth curves. The advantage of a simple approach, such as gain scores, is that they are easy to explain to external stakeholders. The disadvantage is that the scores may not be reliable or valid indicators of an institution's contribution to student learning and development. More complex measures sacrifice ease of interpretability for greater reliability and validity.

The concluding column in this collection was a feature article in *Assessment Update* written by Trudy Banta and me. The column looks back to an article written in 1984 by Jonathan Warren, titled "The Blind Alley of Value Added." Like Warren, we argued that value added, while appealing, could do more harm than good. Our conclusions were based on research that raised questions about the reliability of value-added measures, whether the measures accurately represent student learning, and whether the choice of statistical methods could substantially alter conclusions about institutional effectiveness. Our column concludes with the observation that value added may be a more appropriate concept for representing content learning in the disciplines than for representing the development of generic abilities during college.

A Concluding Note

Over the past two decades, the assessment of generic skills has undergone considerable evolution. Tests of general education, writing, and critical thinking have become more sophisticated, progressing from simple recognition measures to complex constructed-response, production measures. An outcome of these efforts has been highly reliable assessments that are authentic in that they directly assess what students should know and be able to do as a result of a college education. Despite many years of progress, a substantial concern remains—are these measures sensitive to the effects of education programs? Although statistical techniques can be used to tease out relationships between program participation and learning gains, they cannot be effective if the measures themselves are not sensitive to program outcomes. A recurring theme of several columns in this collection is that popular methods for assessing student learning may be better suited to evaluate the effects of education programs in the disciplines than to evaluate an institution's contributions to the development of generic skills, such as critical thinking, communicating, and problem solving.

References

Baird, L. L. (1988). "Diverse and Subtle Arts: Assessing the Generic Outcomes of Higher Education." In C. Adelman (ed.), *Performance and Judgment: Essays on Principles and Practices in the Assessment of College Student Learning* (pp. 39–62). Washington, DC: U.S. Government Printing Office. Document No. OR88-514.

Banta, T. W., Lambert, E. W., Pike, G. R., Schmidhammer, J. L., and Schneider, J. A. (1987). "Estimated Student Score Gain on the ACT COMP Exam: Valid Tool for Institutional Assessment? *Research in Higher Education, 27,* 195–217.

Forrest, A., and Steele, J. M. (1982). *Defining and Measuring General Education Knowledge and Skills.* Iowa City, IA: American College Testing Program.

McCollum, D. (November, 2010). "From Top to Bottom: A Broad and Deep Assessment for the Judicious Use of EPP, CAAP, and CLA. Presentation at the Assessment Institute in Indianapolis.

National Educational Goals Panel. (1991). *The National Education Goals Panel: Building a Nation of Learners.* Washington, DC: U.S. Government Printing Office.

Pike, G. R. (1992). "The Components of Construct Validity: A Comparison of Two Measures of General Education." *Research in Higher Education, 41,* 130–150.

U.S. Department of Education. (2006). *A Test of Leadership: Charting the Future of U.S. Higher Education.*

General Education Assessment

Instruments for Assessing General Education Outcomes

In the 1980s, a wide variety of commercially available tests were used to assess general education outcomes. Some instruments were developed specifically for general education assessment (e.g., Academic Profile, CAAP, College BASE, and COMP), whereas others were developed for other purposes (e.g., ACT, SAT, and CLEP). Although these tests were widely used, relatively little information was available about their appropriateness as measures of general education outcomes. From Assessment Update 1:1 (1989).

During the last two years there has been tremendous growth in the number of institutions interested in assessing the outcomes of general education and in the types of instruments available to assess those outcomes. A brief review of the literature on outcomes research reveals that prior to 1987 five tests were available for general education assessment: the ACT Assessment Program examinations, the College-Level Examination Program (CLEP) General Examinations, the College Outcome Measures Project (COMP) examination, the Graduate Record Examinations (GRE), and the Scholastic Aptitude Test (SAT). Since 1987, four new tests have been introduced: the Academic Profile, the College Basic Academic Subjects Examination (College BASE), the Collegiate Assessment of Academic Proficiency (CAAP), and the Education Assessment Series (EAS) examinations.

In this report I shall provide an overview of each of these tests that will include a brief description of each and an analysis of its strengths and weaknesses. Also included is a listing of the test publishers in case readers want to obtain additional information.

All but one of the tests in use prior to 1987 were designed for some purpose other than evaluating general education programs. For example, the ACT Assessment Program is a battery of college entrance and placement examinations. While research shows that students' scores on these tests predict performance during the first two years of college, there is no consistent evidence that the tests are sensitive to the effects of college coursework.

Likewise, the Scholastic Aptitude Test is designed for use as a college entrance and placement examination, and the quantitative and verbal subscales have been shown to predict performance in college. Publishers of the SAT describe these exams as measures of problem-solving ability; however, there is no evidence that they are particularly sensitive to the effects of general education coursework.

The College-Level Examination Program (CLEP) General Examinations are designed to assess students' knowledge and skills in five content areas. While all five tests are highly reliable and have been linked to student performance in introductory courses in each content area, empirical data on the validity of the CLEP General Examinations as measures of program effectiveness currently are not available.

A test usually given at the end of the undergraduate years, the General Test of the Graduate Record Examinations (GRE), has also been used in assessing the effectiveness of the general education curriculum. The GRE is a nationally-normed exam designed to measure skills that are gained over a long time period and are unrelated to a particular field of study. While this test is most often used to measure students' abilities for graduate study, recent studies conducted by the Differential Coursework Patterns Project funded by the Office of Educational Research and Improvement (OERI) have shown that the nine item types of the GRE General Test are sensitive to the effects of undergraduate coursework.

Of the five tests available prior to 1987, only the College Outcome Measures Project (COMP) examination was designed specifically to measure the outcomes of general education programs. Available both as an Objective Test and as a longer Composite Examination, the COMP exam provides a total score, three content subscores, and three process subscores; the Composite Examination also provides several measures of reasoning and communicating. While research by ACT shows that this exam is sensitive to general education program quality, studies at several institutions indicate that the exam is much more sensitive to individual differences and that the effects attributable to individual differences may mask program effects.

All four of the instruments developed since 1987 are designed to assess general education outcomes. The Academic Profile, for example, is intended to measure four academic skills across three content areas. Results of pilot testing during the 1987–1988 academic year indicated extremely high intercorrelations among the subscales. As a result, a new version of this test has been prepared for administration during the 1988–1989 academic year.

The Collegiate Assessment of Academic Proficiency (CAAP) is intended to measure skills typically attained during the first two years of college. This test consists of four modules that can be administered individually or in combination. In addition, a writing sample based on two independent prompts can be substituted for the multiple choice writing skills module. Because this instrument is just beginning its pilot testing phase, information on reliability and validity is not available.

In the spring of 1988, the College Board introduced the Education Assessment Series (EAS) examinations. Designed to measure learning during the first two years of college, the EAS consists of two tests: one in English composition and one in mathematics. Although the EAS tests are in the developmental stage, national norms are being developed to allow institutions to compare the performance of their students with the performance of students across the country.

It is worth noting that the eight examinations described above are norm-referenced. In contrast, the College Basic Academic Subjects

Examination (College BASE) is a criterion-referenced achievement test. In addition, national norms will be offered for comparative purposes. College BASE is available in a variety of forms, each with different skill reports. At a minimum, scores will be available in several subject areas, and each subject area will have competency and skill subscores. To date, information on the reliability and validity of College BASE is not available.

In sum, at least nine tests are available for use as general education assessment instruments. Unfortunately, the widespread availability of these measures has not been paralleled by extensive research on their reliability and validity as assessment tools. Institutions interested in assessing general education outcomes using one or more of these measures should proceed cautiously, first determining the extent to which the test matches general education curricula, then empirically evaluating the reliability and validity of test scores.

The College Outcome Measures Program (COMP) Examination

The College Outcome Measures Program (COMP) exam was one of the first tests specifically designed for general education assessment. Two forms of the COMP exam were available: the Objective Test, consisting of multiple-choice questions, and the Composite Examination, which included multiple-choice items and exercises requiring students to write essays and record speeches. Many institutions were attracted to the COMP exam because it provided a measure of how much students grew intellectually (i.e., value added) over the course of a college education. From Assessment Update 4:1 (1992).

In 1976 the American College Testing (ACT) Program organized the College Outcome Measures Program (COMP) to develop a measure of "knowledge and skills relevant to successful functioning in adult society"

(Forrest, 1982, p. 11). Available since 1979–1980, the COMP exam has been administered at least once at more than 500 colleges, and it is used annually by approximately 100 four-year institutions in the evaluation of their general education programs. COMP staff acknowledge that the examination is not appropriate for all institutions. They indicate that the COMP exam is most appropriate for evaluating general education programs designed to foster the development of generic higher order cognitive processes, as opposed to discipline-specific or content-specific outcomes (Steele, 1991a).

Since 1983, the COMP exam has been used in Tennessee to evaluate the general education programs of stale colleges and universities and to award millions of dollars in public funds for higher education. Until recently, the COMP exam was the only instrument designed for evaluating general education programs, and in 1992, it remains the only measure for which a substantial amount of data is available.

The COMP exam is available in two forms: the Objective Test (consisting of multiple-choice items) and the Composite Examination (containing multiple-choice questions along with exercises requiring students to write essays and record speeches). ACT reports that the correlation between scores on the Objective Test and Composite Examination is .80, allowing the Objective Test to serve as a proxy for the Composite Examination (Forrest and Steele, 1982). COMP staff recommend that the Composite Examination be used to evaluate the performance of individuals and that the Objective Test be used to evaluate general education programs (Steele, 1991c). Most institutions, including the public colleges and universities in Tennessee, use the Objective Test for program evaluation because it is easier to administer and score.

The Objective Test takes approximately 2½ hours to administer and contains 60 questions, each with two correct answers. The questions are divided among 15 separately timed activities drawing on material (stimuli) from television programs, radio broadcasts, and print media. Students taking the COMP Objective Test are instructed that there is a penalty for guessing (that is, incorrect answers will be subtracted from their scores), but that leaving an answer blank will not be counted against them (Forrest and Steele, 1982).

The combination of two correct answers for each question, the guessing penalty, and no penalty for not answering a question means that the score range for each question is from -2 to 2 points. A score of -2 represents two incorrect answers, while a score of -1 represents one incorrect answer and one answer left blank. A score of 0 represents either both answers left blank or one correct and one incorrect answer. A score of 1 represents one correct answer and one answer left blank, while a score of 2 represents two correct answers. To improve the interpretability of scores, they are rescaled (0–4), making the maximum possible score on the Objective Test 240 points and a chance score 120 points.

New forms of the Objective Test are developed on an annual basis. To ensure the comparability of scores across forms, the COMP staff equates each new form to the original test (Form III). This equating is performed using samples of high school and college seniors who are double-tested using the new form and a previous form of the Objective Test. Statistical procedures involve the use of Angoff's Design II method (J. M. Steele, personal communication, September 14, 1989).

In addition to a total score, the COMP Objective Test provides three content subscores (Functioning Within Social Institutions, Using Science and Technology, and Using the Arts) and three process subscores (Communicating, Solving Problems, and Clarifying Values). In the technical manual for the COMP exam, ACT staff report that the alpha reliability (internal consistency) of the total score is .84 for individuals, and that alpha reliability estimates for the subscores range from .63 to .68 (Forrest and Steele, 1982). Estimates of parallel-forms reliability are .79 for the COMP total score and range from .53 to .68 for the subscores. Most recently, the COMP staff have reported that the generalizability (reliability) coefficients for institution means exceed .90 (for total score and subscores) when the means are based on samples of at least 200 students (Steele, 1989; 1991b).

Many colleges and universities are drawn to the COMP exam because it provides objective evidence of student intellectual growth (value-added) over the course of a college education. Students who persist at an institution can be tested on entrance and again at the end of two or four years of college to determine the growth attributable to their educational experiences (Forrest, 1982).

Partly because many institutions are unwilling to wait two or four years to evaluate student learning, COMP staff provide an estimate of student gain. Based on the fact that the correlation between freshman total scores on the Objective Test and entering ACT Assessment composite scores is .70, the COMP staff have constructed a concordance table from which institutions may estimate mean freshman COMP scores based on ACT Assessment composite scores. By subtracting estimated freshman score means from actual senior COMP score means, an estimate of score gain (value-added) can be obtained.

References

Forrest, A. (1982). *Increasing Student Competence and Persistence: The Best Case for General Education.* Iowa City, IA: ACT National Center for the Advancement of Educational Practice.

Forrest, A., and Steele, J. M. (1982). *Defining and Measuring General Education Knowledge and Skills.* Iowa City, IA: American College Testing Program.

Steele, J. M. *College Outcome Measures Program (COMP): A Generalizability Analysis of the COMP Objective Test (Form 9).* Unpublished manuscript, College Outcome Measures Program, Iowa City, IA.

Steele, J. M. (1991a). *Assessing General Education Outcomes of College.* Unpublished manuscript, College Outcome Measures Program, Iowa City, IA.

Steele, J. M. (1991b). *College Outcome Measures Program (COMP): A Generalizability Analysis of the COMP Objective Test (Form 10).* Unpublished manuscript, College Outcome Measures Program, Iowa City, IA.

Steele, J. M. (1991c). *Evidence for What? Fitting Assessment to the User.* Unpublished manuscript, College Outcome Measures Program, Iowa City, IA.

Joint Task Force of the Interinstitutional Committee of Academic Officers and State Board for Community College Education

The report of Washington State's Joint Task Force represented one of the first attempts to evaluate the accuracy and appropriateness of several standardized tests as measures of the general outcomes of college. The task force concluded that the three measures evaluated (Academic Profile, CAAP, and COMP) were not appropriate for assessing communication, computation and critical thinking. The task force noted that the tests did not appear to be sensitive to the effects of the college experience, and norms for making comparisons with peer institutions were not generally available. From Assessment Update 1:3 (1989).

The Washington State institutions of higher education have a long-standing commitment to assessing student learning and discerning the value of a college education. They agree that assessment helps enhance the quality of programs. Faculty and administrators across the state are currently involved in discussions and studies to determine the best methods for obtaining appropriate and useful information from assessment activities.

Some states use standardized tests to measure students' academic performance. The state Higher Education Coordinating (HEC) Board recommended in its master plan (Dec. 1987) that two-year and four-year institutions conduct a pilot study to evaluate the appropriateness of using standardized tests as one means for measuring the communication, computation, and critical-thinking skills of sophomores. The purposes of such a testing program would be for institutions to strengthen their curricula, improve teaching and learning, and provide accountability data to the public.

To design and implement the study requested by the master plan, two task forces were established. One represented the public baccalaureate institutions, and the other represented the community colleges. Both task forces included faculty and academic administrators from each participating institution, as well as two HEC Board members. The two task forces worked in parallel and ultimately conducted a joint study.

Only three tests met the criteria of the HEC Board's recommendation for study: the Academic Profile, the College Outcome Measures Program (COMP), and the Collegiate Assessment of Academic Proficiency (CAAP). Over 1,300 sophomores from public four-year institutions and from eight two-year colleges were tested, and each student took two of the three tests. More than 100 faculty members from the same institutions took shortened versions of the tests and critiqued them for appropriateness of content and usefulness.

The results of the pilot study strongly suggest that the three tests do not provide an appropriate or useful assessment of the communication, computation, and critical-thinking skills of Washington college sophomores. None of the tests measured the separate academic skills (communication, computation, and critical thinking); rather, these tests primarily measured verbal and quantitative aptitude. Moreover, the tests added little reliable new information about students' academic performance. Results essentially reiterated what is already known from admissions test data and grades. Further, test scores were not sensitive to specific aspects of the college experience, such as estimated time spent studying and credits earned. Finally, none of the tests was judged by faculty as providing an adequate match with curricular content or as being an appropriate or useful measure of communication, computation, and critical thinking.

Norms for making comparisons with peer institutions are currently unavailable. Furthermore, student performance is affected by differences in how institutions administer tests, in the timing of tests, in the selection of students, and in student motivation. Thus, comparisons with future norms which are based on tests given under differing conditions will be misleading.

Analyses of the costs associated with conducting the pilot study suggests that the projected expense of statewide implementation (testing either a sample of sophomores or all sophomores) would be high and would probably exceed the value of the results.

Both two-year and four-year faculty participants in the study recognized the importance and value of having public as well as institutional access to appropriate measures of student performance. They reaffirmed the value of assessment activities for strengthening the curriculum, improving teaching and learning, and enhancing overall instructional quality. They also shared the view that the development of meaningful assessment measures is both difficult and time-consuming, that measures should be institution-specific, and that national standardized multiple-choice tests have serious limitations for the assessment of teaching and learning.

Criteria for Evaluating Assessment Instruments

In this column, construct validity is proposed as a framework for evaluating assessment instruments. Three key questions flow from the construct-validity paradigm: Does the content of the test adequately represent the learning outcomes to be assessed? Is the scoring model (i.e., scales and subscales) consistent with the outcomes being assessed? Are the test scores related to other measures of students' educational experiences and not related to factors beyond an institution's control? From Assessment Update 1:4 (1989).

Washington's Joint Task Force has reported its efforts to evaluate three tests in general education (see my column in the last issue), and similar studies have been conducted at the University of Tennessee. Unfortunately, these studies have been conducted on an ad hoc basis and have not provided a set of standards or a methodology for evaluating assessment instruments.

My purpose in this column is to suggest one possible set of standards for evaluating the appropriateness of using achievement tests as assessment instruments. These standards can be applied to tests in general education or in the major, whether they are commercially available or locally developed.

I propose the use of the concept of validity to evaluate assessment instruments. *Validity* refers to the accuracy and appropriateness of test scores and their interpretations and use. Traditionally, validity has been divided into three types: content, construct, and criterion-related. Today, many measurement scholars, such as Samuel Messick, argue that construct validity provides an all-inclusive methodology for examining score interpretation and use.

When colleges and universities undertake validity studies, the focus of their investigations is score *use*. Judgments about the validity of score meanings are important, but postsecondary institutions are first and foremost users of test information. Their primary concern must be with the appropriateness and consequences of *actions* taken on the basis of test data.

Before any judgments about the validity of score use can be made, colleges and universities must define the constructs that test scores should represent Such concepts as effectiveness and quality must be defined in relationship to the mission and goals of the institution. Since outcomes to be assessed are inherent in the mission and goals, the constructs represented by test scores will, to some extent, be peculiar to each institution.

Once constructs have been identified, a variety of approaches can be used to evaluate their relationships to score use. Three criteria that I have used to evaluate the validity of assessment instruments are the substantive, structural, and external components of construct validity, as described by Jane Loevinger.

The *substantive* component of construct validity focuses on how well test items are accounted for by a construct. Content representativeness and dependability of measurement are important aspects of this component. Samuel Messick notes that a trade-off frequently occurs between content representativeness and dependability of measurement because attempts to faithfully represent all aspects of a construct can result in inclusion of items with large errors of measurement. Conversely, attempts to develop highly reliable tests frequently result in omission of important content areas.

The *structural* component of construct validity focuses on the extent to which relationships among test items accurately reflect the structure of the construct. Al the item level, this component deals with the appropriateness of the scoring model used to represent the construct. At a more general level, the focus is on whether relationships among subscales are consistent with the assumed structure of the construct.

Research related to the *external* component of construct validity focuses on the extent to which relationships between test scores and other measures are consistent with theories of the construct. For example, measures of program quality should be related to measures of educational experience (coursework and involvement) and relatively insensitive to factors beyond the control of colleges and universities (background characteristics).

Although a variety of research techniques can be used to evaluate these three components of construct validity, I have found that comparing test content to an institution's curriculum and goals provides an excellent test of content representativeness. Because there is a potential trade-off between content coverage and dependability, it is advisable to assess the reliability or generalizability of test scores. Factor-analysis procedures (either exploratory or confirmatory) provide a good test of the structural component of construct validity, and structural equations can be used to assess the relationships among scores and external variables.

Suggested Readings

Feldt, L. S., and Brennan, R. L. (1989). "Reliability." In R. L. Linn (ed.), *Educational Measurement*. (3rd. ed., pp. 105–146). New York: Macmillan.

Loevinger, J. (1957). "Objective Tests as Instruments of Psychological Theory." *Psychological Reports, 3*, 635–694.

Messick, S. (1989). "Validity." In R. L. Linn (ed). *Educational Measurement*. (3rd ed., pp. 13–104). New York: Macmillan.

The College Basic Academic Subjects Examination

The College Basic Academic Subjects Examination (College BASE) represented a significant departure from previous measures of general education outcomes. Earlier measures (e.g., Academic Profile, CAAP, and COMP) were norm-referenced in that they evaluated a student or institution's performance against the performance of other students and institutions. College BASE was developed as a criterion-referenced examination which evaluated a student's or institution's performance against predefined standards. From Assessment Update 3:1 (1991).

The College Basic Academic Subjects Examination (College BASE) is one of the newest standardized tests designed for the assessment of general education outcomes. Unlike other tests of this genre, such as the COMP and CAAP exams, the College BASE is a criterion-referenced achievement lest that focuses on the degree to which students have mastered particular skills and competencies commensurate with the completion of general education coursework. College BASE is appropriate for assessing either students or programs. Consequently, the test has been used lo evaluate academic programs at a variety of institutions, and it has been used as a selection criterion for entry into teacher education in Missouri.

College BASE assesses achievement in four subject areas: English, mathematics, science, and social studies. Subject-area scores are built on content clusters, which in turn are based on enabling skills. For example, mathematics scores are based on three content clusters: general mathematics, algebra, and geometry. The cluster score for geometry is derived from skills related to the recognition of two- and three-dimensional figures and the ability to perform geometric calculations. Numerical scores are provided for each subject area and cluster, along with a composite (total) score. Ratings of "high," "medium," or "low" are provided for each enabling skill.

In addition to the evaluation of content areas, the College BASE assesses three competencies across disciplines: interpretive reasoning, strategic reasoning, and adaptive reasoning. According to the test's authors, interpretive reasoning is the most basic level of information processing, beyond factual recall, and includes such abilities as paraphrasing, summarizing, and explaining. In contrast, strategic reasoning includes skills related to definition, comparison, and classification. Adaptive reasoning includes skills related to definition, comparison, and classification. Adaptive reasoning includes the skills of synthesis and evaluation.

The College BASE is available in three forms. The long form includes all four content areas and takes approximately 2½ hours to administer. The short form includes only English and mathematics and can be administered in one hour and twenty minutes. The third form is an institutional-matrix form and takes approximately 40 minutes per student to administer. Written essays may be included with all three forms. The long and short forms of the exam are appropriate for both individual and institutional assessment, while the institutional-matrix form provides only institutional scores.

Item responses on the College BASE are calibrated and scaled with a two-parameter logistical item-response model. The scale for the composite (total) score, as well as for the subject, cluster, and competency scores, has a mean of 300 and a range of from 40 to 560 points. The standard deviation for each score is set at 65 points. Students' performance on the test closely parallels its specifications. For example, a score of 299 represents the 50th percentile on the test, compared to a theoretical mean of 300 points.

The authors of the test report that KR-20 estimates of the reliability (internal consistency) of scores on the cross-disciplinary College BASE range from .77 (English) to .89 (mathematics) for the subject-area scores. These estimates for the cluster scores range from .73 (adaptive reasoning) to .86 (strategic reasoning).

A recent study of the dependability of group means on the College BASE conducted at the University of Tennessee, Knoxville (UTK), found that institutional scores on the test are quite dependable, even when they are based on relatively small samples of students. For example, samples of 50 students' generalizability coefficients for all four subject-area scores are in excess of .90.

As evidence of the validity of the College BASE, its authors have conducted factor analysis of test scores that have reproduced the subscales specified on the test. Analyses of College BASE scores also indicate that the test has significant positive correlations with students' scores on the ACT Assessment examination, Scholastic Achievement Test (SAT), and cumulative grade point average, the authors say. Research on the administration of the test to more than 1,000 students at UTK provides additional evidence of test validity. First, factor analysis of the nine cluster scores on the long form of the test reproduced the test's four subject-area scores. Second, analysis of the relationships between students' subject-area scores and their coursework in history, humanities, mathematics, natural science, and social science revealed that coursework in mathematics was significantly related to mathematics scores, natural science coursework to science scores, and history coursework to social studies scores. Counter to expectations, humanities coursework was not significantly related to English scores.

Overall, our experiences with the College BASE at UTK indicate that this test is the most appropriate standardized test we have investigated for evaluating the effects of our general education program. Its strengths lie in the number of specific subscores provided, the evidence of the construct validity of those subscores, and the relationship of content areas to specific patterns of coursework. Despite these strengths, an evaluation of the test content by a faculty committee revealed that the test covers only about 36% of the general education goals at UTK. Thus, while this test may be the most appropriate standardized test for UTK, it suffers the same limitation as other standardized tests do in that it covers only a fraction of UTK's general education outcomes. Faculty at any other institution considering the College BASE would need to compare its stated outcomes for general education with the specifications developed for the exam, in order to determine the appropriateness of the College BASE for its own purposes. It is generally accepted, however, that any standardized test used for assessment should be supplemented by other measures, such as essays and performance appraisals.

As a concluding note, it should be emphasized that the results for UTK are specific to our institution and should not be taken as an indication of the validity of the College BASE at any other institution. Nevertheless, the results do suggest that institutions interested in using standardized tests to assess general education outcomes should give serious consideration to the College BASE.

For Further Reference

Center for Educational Assessment, University of Missouri–Columbia. (1988). *College BASE*. Chicago: Riverside Publishing.

Osterlind, S. J. (1989). *College BASE: Guide to Test Content*. Chicago: Riverside Publishing.

Osterlind, S. J. (1990). *College BASE Technical Manual*. Chicago: Riverside Publishing.

Pike, G. R. (1992). "The Components of Construct Validity: A Comparison of Two
· Measures of General Education Outcomes." *Journal of General Education, 41*, 130–150.

The Academic Profile II

The Academic Profile and the Academic Profile II were widely used by colleges and universities to assess the quality and effectiveness of their general education programs. Introduced in 1989, the Academic Profile II offered several improvements over the original test. These improvements included superior psychometric properties, a 40-minute short form that could be administered in a single class period, and the ability to select peers (for norming) from a list of user institutions. From Assessment Update 3:5 *(1991).*

During 1987–88 the Educational Testing Service (ETS) introduced the *Academic Profile*, a test of academic skills designed to assist colleges and universities in assessing the quality and effectiveness of their general education programs. During the first two years of pilot testing, the *Academic Profile* was used by more than 200 two- and four- year institutions to test over 60,000 students.

The original version of the *Academic Profile* was available in both short and long forms. The long form provided reliable scores for both individuals and groups, and measured four types of skills (reading, writing, critical thinking, and mathematics) in three content areas (humanities, social sciences, and natural sciences). Highly reliable total scores were also provided for both individuals and groups. The short form of the exam provided reliable group scores for the four skill areas and three content areas, as well as reliable total scores for both individuals and groups. An optional written essay was available with both forms of the exam.

Based on two years of pilot testing, ETS identified several problems with the original version of the *Academic Profile*, as well as several opportunities for improved score reporting. In 1989–90 ETS began pilot testing a new version of the test, the *Academic Profile II*. Changes in the test included significantly lower intercorrelations among the four skills dimensions and a 40-minute short form that could be administered in a standard class period. Also, ETS began using scaled scores for total score and the seven subscores.

Related to the first change, factor analyses identified three factors as being measured in the skill areas: writing, mathematics, and reading/critical thinking. The factor structure of the *Academic Profile II* allowed development of several new performance-level (criterion-referenced) indicators. For the long form of the exam, seven performance indicators are provided: writing, mathematics, reading/critical thinking (combined), reading/critical thinking (humanities), reading/critical thinking (social sciences), and reading/critical thinking (natural sciences) . Three performance indicators are available to users of the short form: writing, mathematics, and reading/critical thinking (combined). Three levels of performance are described for each indicator.

To assist institutions in interpreting score information, two types of comparative (norm-referenced) data are provided. First, *Standard Reference Group* reports that aggregate the mean scores of all institutions testing at least 30 students in a given year are provided for total score, the four skill subscores, and the three content subscores. Second, institutions may select a group of peers from a list of user institutions and *Self-Selected Reference Group* reports are provided for total score and subscores.

In addition to the multiple-choice questions on the long and short forms of the new *Academic Profile II*, several demographic questions are included and a 45-minute essay is available on an optional basis. Institutions can add up to 50 locally developed multiple-choice items to the test.

The technical manual for the *Academic Profile II* indicates that the reliability of total score on the long form for individuals is .94, and reliability estimates for the skills and content subscores range from .74 (critical thinking) to .85 (reading). Reliability of total score on the short form for individuals is .80. Reliability estimates for institutional mean scores on the long form are .99 for total score and all subscores. Reliability estimates for institutional means on the short form are somewhat lower. They range from .88 (social sciences) to .95 (mathematics). The group mean reliability coefficient for total score on the short form is .90.

The technical manual also reports the results of three analyses designed to evaluate the construct validity of total scores and the seven norm-referenced subscores on the *Academic Profile II*. Specifically, the research indicates that total scores and subscores are significantly higher for students with a cumulative grade point average above 3.00 (on a 4-point scale) than for students with grade point averages below 3.00. Research on score differences by class rank (freshman, sophomore, junior, and senior) also generally supported the validity of scores on the *Academic Profile II*. In some cases, however, means for adjacent categories (such as, sophomore vs. junior) were not significantly different. Relationships between skill and content scores by proportion of the core curriculum completed also indicated that these scores are positively related to quantity of coursework.

As previously noted, factor analysis of item-type scores from the *Academic Profile* II indicates the existence of three underlying factors corresponding to writing, mathematics, and reading/critical thinking. The results are presented by ETS as evidence of the construct validity of the criterion-referenced proficiency level scores on the test. The test developers also indicate that slightly over two-thirds of the students they sampled showed differentiation in their proficiency scores. That is, two-thirds of the students had different levels of performance depending on the proficiency score being considered. The authors of the technical manual conclude that these results provide evidence of the discriminant validity of the proficiency scores.

References

College Board and Educational Testing Service. (1990). *The Academic Profile: User's Guide*. Princeton, NJ: College Board and Educational Testing Service.
College Board and Educational Testing Service. (1990). *Higher Education Assessment Newsletter*. Princeton, NJ: College Board and Educational Testing Service.

The Collegiate Learning Assessment

The Collegiate Learning Assessment (CLA) represents a significant departure from traditional general education assessments because it requires students to produce artifacts that are evaluated using a set of scoring rubrics. The CLA provides institution-level scores for first-year students and seniors, as well as a measure of value added for each group. The test developers report high levels of inter-rater agreement in scoring students' products. Also, value-added measures have been found to vary across institutions. From Assessment Update 18:2 (2006).

Several measures of the general outcomes of college are commercially available today. Most of these assessments—the Collegiate Assessment of Academic Proficiency (CAAP), College Basic Academic Subjects Examination (College BASE), and Measure of Academic Proficiency and Progress (MAPP)—are recognition measures; that is, they evaluate students' ability to recognize the correct answers on multiple-choice tests. Although all three of these tests include optional writing tasks, the primary emphasis of the assessments is on recognition. The Collegiate Learning Assessment (CLA) represents a departure from traditional recognition measures. Students who participate in the CLA are required to produce artifacts that are evaluated based on a set of scoring criteria or rubrics. These production measures are frequently referred to as *direct assessments of student learning*. The CLA also differs from other commercially available instruments in that its score reporting focuses on the value added by college.

In this column, I will provide a general overview of the CLA, including the types of measures included in the assessment, and discuss administration, score reports, and information on the psychometric properties of the assessment. The next column in this series will present the experiences of one institution with the CLA, and a third column will address issues related to using value-added models to evaluate institutional quality and effectiveness.

Content

Developed by the Council for Aid to Education (CAE) and the RAND Corporation, the CLA requires students to analyze information and give written responses to a series of questions. The CLA includes two types of measures: (1) a performance task and (2) writing prompts. The performance task requires that students complete what is frequently termed an *authentic activity*, such as preparing a memorandum or a policy recommendation. There are three parts to the task. The first part provides students with introductory or background material about the task. The second part of the assessment is a library of documents that the students can use in completing the task. The third part of the assessment consists of a series of questions students must answer in completing the task.

In the publication *Collegiate Learning Assessment: CLA in Context*, CAE provides the following background information for a sample performance task: "You advise Pat Williams, the president of DynaTech, a company that makes precision electronic instruments and navigational equipment. Sally Evans, a member of DynaTech's sales force, recommended that DynaTech buy a small private plane (a SwiftAir 235) that she and other members of the sales force could use to visit customers. Pat was about to approve the purchase when there was an accident involving a Swiftair 235."

The following documents would be available to students: "(1) newspaper article about the accident, (2) Federal Accident Report on in-flight breakups in single-engine planes, (3) internal correspondence (Pat's e-mail to you and Sally's e-mail to Pat), (4) charts relating to SwiftAir's performance characteristics, (5) excerpt from a magazine article comparing SwiftAir 235 to similar planes, (6) pictures and descriptions of SwiftAir models 180 and 235."

The performance task includes the following questions: "Do the available data tend to support or refute the claim that the type of wing on the SwiftAir 235 leads to more in-flight breakups? What is the basis for your conclusion? What other factors might have contributed to the accident and should be taken into account? What is your preliminary recommendation about whether or not DynaTech should buy the plane and what is the basis for this recommendation?"

In addition to the performance task, the CLA includes two analytic writing tasks. The first, a "make-an-argument" task, requires students to write an essay in support of or in opposition to a statement such as "There is no such thing as 'truth' in the media. The one true thing about the information media is that it exists only to entertain." Students are told that they can take any position, as long as they provide reasons for their position and support their arguments. The second writing task requires students to critique an argument. Students are given an argument—for example, a description of an elementary school principal who uses information from a study linking fast food restaurants and childhood obesity to oppose opening fast food restaurants near the school. Students taking the CLA are then asked to evaluate the reasoning in the argument.

Administration and Score Reports

The CLA is designed to be administered to samples of 100 first-year students and 100 seniors. In 2004–05, first-year students completed the assessment in the fall and seniors completed the assessment in the winter or spring. During the 2004–05 academic year, first-year students completed both the performance task and the writing prompts, a three-hour assessment. To reduce administration time, seniors responded to either the performance task or the two writing prompts.

In administering the CLA, institutions must first identify appropriate samples of students, recruit the students to participate in the assessment, proctor the assessment in a computer lab with Internet access, and provide CAE with registrar data, including students' ACT and SAT scores. The cost of administering the CLA to 100 first-year and 100 senior students is $6,300. Additional students can be tested at a cost of $20 per student. Institutions can also conduct four-year longitudinal studies of their students for $28,000.

A variety of reports is available from CAE. Students receive individual score reports by the end of the quarter or semester in which they participate in the assessment. The individual score report provides students with information about how they performed relative to students who completed the same test. Institutions can receive copies of the student score reports if students give their permission. Campuses also receive two institutional reports. The first report is sent in midwinter and provides information on the performance of incoming first-year students. The second report on seniors' performance is available in early summer.

Score reports for first-year students and seniors focus on value-added analysis. Two different value-added measures are included in score reports. The first value-added measure is based on deviation scores and is provided for both first-year students and seniors. The deviation score indicates the extent to which students at an institution have higher or lower CLA scores than would be expected based on the students' admission test scores (ACT and SAT scores). The deviation scores are residual scores derived from a model in which all participating students' CLA scores are regressed on ACT and SAT scores. Based on charts in the CAE publication *Collegiate Learning Assessment: Institutional Report*, it appears that separate regression analyses are conducted for first-year students and seniors. In the institutional report, deviation scores are provided for the institution, not individual students. In this case, the institution's deviation score would be the mean of student deviation scores.

The second value-added measure is presented in the institutional report for seniors. This measure represents the difference between the deviation score for seniors and the deviation score for first-year students. Again, the institution serves as the unit of analysis, and the institutional difference score is compared with difference scores for other participating institutions. Examples of the information provided in CLA score reports are provided in the CAE publication *Collegiate Learning Assessment: Institutional Report*.

Psychometric Properties

In addition to the previously mentioned publications on context and score reports, the CAE Web site includes articles on the conceptual framework underlying the CLA and a study by Stephen Klein and his colleagues examining the reliability and validity of the measures. The report by Klein and his colleagues indicates that interrater agreement for the scoring of the performance tasks and writing prompts is reasonably high—0.89 on the performance task and 0.86 on the writing prompts. Klein and his colleagues also note that the reliability for a total score based on a performance task and two writing prompts is approximately 0.71. They further note than an institutional mean based on 100 students would yield a group mean generalizability (reliability) coefficient substantially greater than 0.71.

Evidence to date indicates that the relationships between students' entering ACT or SAT test scores and CLA scores are quite strong. For example, the R-square coefficients for the regression of CLA performance task scores on entering test scores were 0.858 for first-year students and 0.789 for seniors. This finding indicates that 85.8 percent of the variance in first-year students' performance-task scores and 78.9 percent of the variance in seniors' performance-task scores can be explained by their entering ability levels. The corresponding correlations between performance-task scores and entering ability scores for first-year students and seniors are 0.926 and 0.888, respectively. Relationships are not as strong for the other CLA measures, but the relationships are still quite substantial, explaining 60–70 percent of the variance in CLA scores (Council for Aid to Education [n.d.]).

Despite the very strong relationship between CLA scores and measures of entering ability, and the relatively small number of institutions participating in the pilot study by Klein and his colleagues, the researchers found statistically significant differences between institutional deviation (residual) scores. No indication of the magnitude of the differences among institutions is provided in the research paper.

Additional information on the Collegiate Learning Assessment is available on the Council for Aid to Education's CLA Web site at <http://www.collegiatelearningassessment.org>.

References

Council for Aid to Education. (n.d). *Collegiate Learning Assessment: CLA in Context.* New York: Council for Aid to Education.

Council for Aid to Education. (n.d). *Collegiate Learning Assessment: Institutional Report.* New York: Council for Aid to Education.

Klein, S., Kuh, G., Chun, M., Hamilton, L., and Shavelson, R. (Apr. 2003). "The Search for Value-Added: Assessing and Validating Selected Higher Education Outcomes." Paper presented at the annual meeting of the American Educational Research Association, Chicago. http://www.cae.org/content/pdf/AERATheSearch ForValueAdded.pdf.

Writing Assessment

Designing Comprehensive Writing Assessments

Experience with statewide writing assessment programs suggests that three questions need to be answered when institutions are designing comprehensive writing assessments. First, should one-shot or process writing assessment be utilized? Second, what type of writing prompt (e.g., narrative, expository, or persuasive) should be used? Third, what type of scoring rubric (i.e., holistic or analytic) should be used? Answers to these questions will define the nature of the writing assessment program. From Assessment Update 5:5 (1993).

Since coming to the Center for Educational Assessment (CEA) in January, one of my major projects has been the statewide assessment of student writing for grades K–12. Because many colleges and universities are interested in assessing the quality of student writing as part of their evaluation of general education programs (or their writing-across-the-curriculum programs), I thought that it might be helpful to recount some of our experiences. In this column I will provide a brief description of the writing assessment program in Missouri and discuss some of the basic questions that must be addressed in developing a writing assessment program. In a subsequent column, I will be discussing some of the findings of recent CEA evaluations of the Missouri Writing Assessment program.

The easiest way to organize this description is to examine three of the key questions that should be answered in order to establish a viable writing assessment program. I want to stress that there are no "right" answers to these questions. However, the ways in which institutions answer them profoundly shape the nature of writing assessment on their campuses.

The first question is "What sort of writing task should be used?" The choice initially is between what I call a one-shot writing assessment and an assessment of the process of writing. In the one-shot assessment, students are given a topic and told that they have a certain amount of time (usually about one hour) to write an essay. This approach is frequently used in commercial general education assessment instruments, such as the Academic Profile and College BASE. The strength of the one-shot method is its ease of administration. Its limitation is that it usually does not reflect the writing process students use.

The alternative, a process-writing approach, is designed to parallel more closely the actual writing process of students. The present Missouri Writing Assessment is an example of the process-writing approach. Students are allotted three class periods in which to write. The first is devoted to prewriting activities and an initial draft. During the second class period, students are encouraged to continue drafting and to begin revising their essays. During the final period, students complete their revisions and prepare a final copy of the essay.

Clearly, the major liability of the process-writing approach is the time required for administration and scoring. Scoring takes longer because the essays tend to be longer. However, the time is well spent. Research conducted by CEA has found that the process-writing approach has much greater face validity with classroom teachers than the one-shot approach. In addition, scores tend to be somewhat higher, and there is greater variability in scores. When a one-shot writing assessment was used in Missouri, it was discovered that 85% of the students received a score of 3 on a six-point scale. With the process-writing approach, slightly less than 40% of the students received a score of 3.

Once the nature of the task has been defined, assessment professionals are confronted with the choice of which type of writing prompt to use (for example, personal narrative, expository essay, or persuasive essay). This choice is not trivial. Several researchers have reported that writing scores vary more across types of writing than across students. In 1992, most students in Missouri wrote expository essays. However, a randomly selected subsample of students wrote personal narratives. Results indicated that students who wrote personal narratives had significantly higher scores than students who wrote expository essays (half a point higher on a six-point scale).

A related issue in selecting writing prompts is whether the topics should be generic or discipline specific. Recently, I have been working with several community colleges that are developing assessment programs. One is implementing writing assessment. In pilot testing the writing assessment, it was discovered that standards for writing were significantly different across the disciplines (sciences, social sciences, humanities, and so on). If institutions elect to use a generic writing prompt, they run the risk of not assessing the kinds of writing performance expected of their students. On the other hand, if an institution administers many different kinds of writing prompts, it may be difficult or impossible to generalize across writing samples and arrive at an overall evaluation of the general education writing program.

Irrespective of the type of prompt selected, the directions should include sufficient introductory material to provide the students with a context for the writing exercise. At a minimum, students need to know the purpose for the essay and the intended audience.

The final question that must be answered in developing a writing assessment concerns the type of scoring rubric to be used. For simplicity I will focus on the choice between holistic and analytical rubrics. Holistic rubrics require raters to make a global evaluation of writing samples based on the assumption that the overall impression conveyed by an essay is greater than the sum of its parts. Analytical scoring rubrics contain multiple scoring scales covering different aspects of writing, such as ideas and content, organization, word choice, sentence structure, voice, and so forth. Many of the final recommendations suggest that holistic approaches be used for summative end-of-term assessment and that analytical approaches be used for formative assessment designed to provide feedback to students.

Despite the ongoing debate over the relative merits of holistic and analytical scoring methods, one fact is clear. Analytical scoring methods are substantially more time-consuming than holistic ones. For example, one study found that it took 2½ times as long to train raters and score essays using analytical methods. At the present time, CEA and the Missouri Department of Elementary and Secondary Education are conducting a study comparing holistic and analytical scoring approaches. The results of that research will be included in a subsequent column on writing assessment.

Implementing a Large-Scale Writing Assessment

The Missouri statewide writing assessment program provides insights into the practical issues associated with designing and implementing large-scale assessments of writing. Many of these practical issues revolve around improving the reliability and the validity of writing scores. Based on the Missouri experience, three principles are identified: (1) there is no substitute for rigor; (2) assessment frequently serves multiple purposes; and (3) assessment must be coupled with feedback to produce improvement in performance. From Assessment Update 6:1 (1994).

In a previous column (*Assessment Update*, 1993, vol. 5, no. 5, pp. 9, 11), I described several issues that should be addressed when developing a writing assessment program. These include questions about the nature of the writing task (one-shot versus process writing), the prompts (personal narrative, expository, persuasive, and so on), and the type of scoring rubric (holistic, analytical, or a combination) to be used.

In this column, I examine some of the practical issues involved in writing assessment, using as an example the statewide writing assessment at grades 5, 8, and 11 in Missouri. While this illustration is drawn from K–12 assessment, the principles outlined can be transferred to higher education assessment.

Missouri introduced statewide direct writing assessment in 1987. From 1987 to 1989, students wrote for one class period on topics that required a personal narrative style of writing. Approximately 30 teachers were trained as raters and scored the writing samples over the summer using a holistic scoring rubric.

Analyses of the Missouri writing assessment from 1987 to 1989 found that the project had little or no discernible effect on the teaching or learning of writing. Based on these results, an advisory committee met to discuss methods of improving writing and writing assessment in Missouri. The outcome of these deliberations was the development of a process-oriented writing assessment that began in 1990. The purposes of the current writing assessment are threefold: (1) to emphasize the importance of writing, (2) to familiarize students and teachers with the process approach to writing, and (3) to provide data on the quality of writing proficiency in Missouri.

The present writing assessment is organized as a three-day writing workshop that models good instruction and pedagogy in order to familiarize teachers with process-oriented writing strategies and to encourage teachers to develop curriculum-embedded writing assessment. Students are allotted three 45-minute class periods to write. The first class period is devoted to prewriting activities and an initial draft. In the second period, students are encouraged to continue drafting and revision activities. During the third class period, students complete the revisions and copy their papers in ink into scannable test booklets.

The Missouri Department of Elementary and Secondary Education (DESE), in conjunction with the Center for Educational Assessment (CEA), coordinates holistic scoring sessions at several sites around the state. Each year a cadre of elementary and secondary school teachers is recruited and trained to score the essays. Two raters read and score each paper independently. A student's score is the average of these two scores. For example, if a student is given a score of 3 by the first rater and of 4 by the second, the final score for that student will be 3.5. When there is more than a 1-point difference in the scores of the two raters, a third rater is asked to read and score the paper. When a third rater is used, the student's score is the average of the two closest scores.

Anchor, training, and certification papers play an important role in the training of raters. These papers are used to familiarize raters with the scoring rubric, provide good examples of each point on the scoring rubric, provide opportunities for raters to employ the rubric prior to the actual scoring sessions, and evaluate whether raters can properly employ the rubric in scoring essays.

Anchor papers are intended to provide the best examples of the score points on the rubric. Initially, DESE and CEA staff meet to select approximately 20 "rough" anchor papers. These are used to train members of the anchor selection committee, which is asked to identify at least 60 papers on which there is strong consensus for inclusion in anchor, training, and certification packets. Papers selected by the committee must have at least 70% agreement on the score for inclusion in certification and training packets. There must be at least 90% agreement on the papers selected for the anchor packets.

Six packets of papers are used to train raters. These packets include two anchor packets representing the score points in the rubric, two practice packets representing most of the score points in the rubric, and two certification packets representing any variety of score points. In addition, the anchor selection committee identifies "red-dot" papers to check the accuracy of raters during the scoring of the Missouri writing assessment.

The training of raters begins with a description of the scoring rubric, and anchor papers are presented as examples of the various score points. Once prospective raters are familiar with the scoring rubric, they are given the practice packets and asked to rate the papers. These practice ratings are discussed and compared to the scores awarded by the anchor selection committee.

Upon completion of the training session, the prospective raters are certified. In order to be certified, a prospective rater must match predetermined scores exactly on at least 50% of the papers and be within one point of the predetermined score on 80% of the papers in the packet. If raters are not certified on the first attempt, they are retrained and recertified. Once certified, raters begin scoring the writing samples.

Red-dot papers are used to maintain the integrity of the rubric during the actual scoring process. A total of four sets of five different red-dot papers is given to raters midway through each of three scoring sessions: the afternoon of the first day, the morning of the second, and the afternoon of the third. Raters score the red-dot papers, and these scores are compared to predetermined scores to evaluate whether decay or drift in scoring has occurred and to identify raters who should be retrained.

When all of the papers have been scored, CEA staff scan the Missouri writing assessment scores electronically, process the data, and return the information to the schools in the form of individual and group summary score reports for specified grade levels. In addition, statewide summaries are prepared for DESE.

This lengthy discussion of K–12 writing assessment in Missouri is warranted not because it is the ideal model for writing assessment but because it illustrates three practical aspects of writing assessment:

Principle 1: There is no substitute for rigor. Too many people seem to feel that subjective performance assessments do not require the same degree of rigor in research methods as do standardized multiple-choice tests. I contend that reliance on subjective evaluations requires greater control because the presence of subjective evaluations adds another source of variance (and possible error) to the assessment process. A clear understanding of the scoring rubric, adequate training, and certification of raters are essential to ensure that score differences reflect differences in students' abilities, not differences in raters.

A concrete example may serve to make this point. In 1993, as part of a special study of the Missouri writing assessment, a subsample of papers from 1992 was rescored using novice raters who were given anchor, training, and certification papers from an earlier prompt. Results indicated that percentages of interrater agreement were much lower in the special study than for the original scoring. In addition, the special-study scores were significantly different from the scores in the original writing assessment. The conclusion from this research was that accurate and reliable scoring of writing assessment requires the use of appropriate anchor, training, and certification materials.

Principle 2: Assessment frequently serves multiple purposes. A corollary of this principle is that multiple purposes produce trade-offs between the goals of the program and methodological rigor. For example, the goals of the Missouri writing assessment include training teachers, improving writing, and obtaining evaluation data. Of these three goals, training teachers in the use and evaluation of process writing is the most important. Excluding teachers from the scoring sessions may improve the reliability of the scoring process, but it does not familiarize teachers with process writing. Consequently, certification standards for raters of the writing samples are significantly lower than the certification standards CEA imposes for *College BASE,* and they are lower than the standards set for other K–12 assessments, such as NAEP. At the same time, research indicates that raters tend to perform to the level of certification (for example, a 50% certification standard translates into 50% interrater agreement). Thus, the decision to set a relatively low certification standard allows virtually all teachers to be certified and to gain experience in evaluating process writing, but it also lowers the reliability of the writing scores.

In any assessment program with multiple goals, certain trade-offs are inevitable. What is important is that assessment leaders explicitly consider these trade-offs as they set priorities and design an assessment program.

Principle 3: Assessment must be coupled with feedback to produce improvements in performance. Early (1987–1989) writing assessments in Missouri used one-shot methods that were not representative of how students write and provided little feedback to students or teachers. It was not surprising that little improvement in writing was found. Subsequent writing assessments have used more authentic methods and provided feedback to students, teachers, and school administrators. For the upcoming writing assessment, both holistic and modified analytical scoring approaches will be used in order to provide students and teachers with additional information about the strengths and weaknesses of students' abilities.

One possible component of the feedback loop is describing and teaching to the rubric. On the surface, this may seem like teaching to the test.

However, if the rubric represents good writing practice, then describing and teaching to the rubric serves to make the standards for assessment (and good writing) clear to the students. While this practice may improve writing scores, it also improves the quality of students' writing.

In summary, the experiences with writing assessment in Missouri should teach us, first, that we must keep the goals of assessment in mind when designing an outcomes assessment program. If the primary goal of the assessment is improvement, procedures must be developed to provide accurate and appropriate training and feedback to students, teachers, and administrators. Whether the goal of an assessment program is accountability or improvement, methodological rigor in the conduct of the assessment is essential.

Critical Thinking Assessment

Assessing the Critical Thinking Abilities of College Students

The ability to think critically is generally considered one of the most important outcomes of a college education. The answers to three questions should be used to guide the development of assessments of critical thinking. First, what is critical thinking? Second, is critical thinking unidimensional or multidimensional? Third, should the development of critical thinking be viewed as a continuum in which the attainment of critical thinking skills is additive, or should development be viewed as a series of stages individuals must pass through? From Assessment Update 8:2 (1996).

We generally take for granted that some of the most important outcomes of a college education are the abilities to think critically, reason effectively, and solve problems. As Pascarella, Terenzini, and their colleagues have observed, disciplinary knowledge becomes obsolete very quickly. Consequently, one of the most lasting contributions a college or university can make is to cultivate enduring critical thinking skills among its students. Given current interest in critical thinking, it is not surprising that the *Campus Trends* surveys conducted by the American Council on Education have consistently found that measurement of students' critical thinking skills plays an important role in most campus assessment programs. Improved critical thinking and problem solving are also important components of the National Education Goals and federal efforts to assess college student learning (see Editor's Notes, p. 3).

Because evaluating students' critical thinking abilities can be an important part of assessing the impact of college on students, I plan to devote several Assessment Measures columns to the topic of assessing critical thinking. In this column, I focus on some of the general issues surrounding critical thinking assessments, then I provide a brief survey of the kinds of assess men i measures that are available. Subsequent columns will focus on specific measures or classes of instruments.

One of the most basic issues surrounding the assessment of *critical thinking* is the definition of this term. As Cuban (1984, p. 676) observed, defining what is meant by critical thinking "is troublesome to both social scientists and practitioners. Troublesome is a polite word; the area is a conceptual swamp." I would venture that most of us would say we can define critical thinking. However, I would also wager that our definitions will vary considerably. Many scholars interested in studying critical thinking resort to a laundry list of skills and abilities to define it. For example, Pascarella and Terenzini (1991, p. 118) concluded that critical thinking "typically involves the individual's ability to do some or all of the following: identify central issues and assumptions in an argument, recognize important relationships, make correct inferences from data, deduce conclusions from information or data provided, interpret whether conclusions are warranted on the basis of the data given, and evaluate evidence or authority." While a listing of critical thinking skills can be helpful, it does not provide a framework from which to view the concept. My own bias is that assessment practitioners need conceptual frameworks (for example, theories of how college affects students) in order to interpret data about student performance and program effectiveness.

From my perspective, one of the more useful conceptual frameworks for viewing critical thinking was proposed by Leonard Baird (1988). Baird's model of college outcomes consists of three interrelated levels: basic skills, general learned abilities, and generic academic outcomes. In Baird's hierarchy, basic skills are fundamental skills that are prerequisite to learning in college. Skills at this level include mastery of the basics of arithmetic and the ability to read and comprehend ordinary paragraphs.

The term for Baird's second level, *general learned abilities*, undoubtedly comes from his years with the Educational Testing Service (ETS). This term consistently appears in descriptions of what the tests developed by ETS purport to measure. These abilities are broader than basic skills and are presumed to underlie basic academic work. Staff at ETS frequently argue that general learned abilities are largely content-free and represent remarkably stable traits that are not easily affected by education programs.

At the apex of Baird's hierarchy are generic academic outcomes: learned abilities that develop as a result of college experiences. Although generic academic outcomes are broader than traditional conceptualizations of critical thinking, higher-order thinking skills are a crucial part of these outcomes, I particularly like the fact that Baird's generic outcomes are the product of a student's total college experiences, not a particular course or group of courses. I also find it intriguing that in Baird's model higher-order thinking skills are at the apex of the hierarchy and sensitive to college effects. In most hierarchical models, the focus lends to be on stable traits at the apex. In Baird's model, those stable traits are at the middle level of the hierarchy.

Another issue in the assessment of higher-order thinking skills concerns whether critical thinking is unidimensional or multidimensional. Given that many different types of abilities (for example, interpretation of evidence, integration of information, and evaluation of conclusions) are included within the critical thinking rubric, it seems likely that a multidimensional representation would be preferred. However, many of the most widely used critical thinking measures are unidimensional, as are most documented college outcomes. It may be that while multidimensional models provide a much richer representation of critical thinking, the outcomes associated with college are essentially unidimensional. Robert L. Thorndike (1985, p. 253) reached a similar conclusion when he reviewed the research on the relationships among job performance, training, and general cognitive ability: "In the context of practical prediction, 'g' appears to be alive and well."

A third issue in assessing critical thinking concerns the nature of student development. For example, should student development be viewed as a continuum in which the attainment of critical thinking abilities is essentially additive, or should development be viewed as a series of stages students pass through as they develop higher-order thinking skills? How this question is answered has a powerful influence on how thinking skills will be measured. When student development is presumed to be continual, traditional objective tests can provide reliable and valid measures of higher-order thinking skills. However, when student development is viewed as a series of discrete stages, traditional objective tests are less useful. In order to provide valid representations of stage development, assessments generally make greater use of expert judgment in assigning individuals to different stages.

How these three issues are addressed can provide a useful heuristic for organizing measures of higher-order thinking skills. For example, one of the most widely used measures of students' critical thinking abilities, the Watson-Glaser Critical Thinking Appraisal, focuses on the types of outcomes described by Pascarella and Terenzini (1991) and is essentially a unidimensional measure of development along a continuum. This test is joined by other standardized objective measures of critical thinking, such as the Cornell Critical Thinking Test and the critical thinking subtest of the Collegiate Assessment of Academic Proficiency.

While many of the traditionally organized unidimensional measures of critical thinking are objective tests, more subjective measures are not automatically excluded from this category. Performance assessments, such as those used in McBer's Comprehensive Cognitive Assessment Battery and the Ennis-Weir Critical Thinking Essay Test, can also yield unidimensional measures of the development of critical thinking skills along a continuum. At the same time, objective measures, such as the Erwin Scale of Intellectual Development, can provide multidimensional representations of students' critical thinking abilities.

Although all of the instruments discussed thus far differ in the types of higher-order thinking skills they assess and how those skills are measured, all of these instruments reflect the belief that growth in critical thinking abilities is additive and occurs along a continuum. Measures such as the Reflective Judgment Interview, Measure of Epistemological Reflection, and even Kohlberg's measure of moral development represent a fundamentally different orientation in the assessment of critical thinking skills. The Reflective Judgment Interview, for example, uses expert judgment and a seven-stage model of thinking skills to assess student performance.

As the preceding discussion indicates, a variety of models are available to explain how college affects critical thinking and to measure critical thinking outcomes. My next column will focus on some of the traditional measures of critical thinking, such as the Watson-Glaser Critical Thinking Appraisal and the critical thinking subtest of the Collegiate Assessment of Academic Proficiency. Subsequent columns will examine alternative ways of measuring higher-order thinking skills, including the Reflective Judgment Interview.

Referenccs

Baird, L. L. (1988). "Diverse and Subtle Arts: Assessing the Generic Outcomes of Higher Education." In C. Adelman (ed.), *Performance and Judgment: Essays on Principles and Practice in the Assessment of College Student Learning.* Washington, DC: Government Printing Office. Document No. OR88-514.

Cuban, L. (1984). "Policy and Research Dilemmas in the Teaching of Reasoning: Unplanned Designs." *Review of Educational Research,* 54, 655–681.

Pascarella. E.T., and Terenzini, P. T. (1991). *How College Affects Students: Findings and Insights from Twenty Years of Research.* San Francisco: Jossey-Bass.

Thorndike, R. L. (1985). "The Central Role of General Ability in Prediction." *Multivariate Behavioral Research,* 20, 241–254.

Suggested Readings

Halpern, D. F. (1994). "A National Assessment of Critical Thinking Skills in Adults: Taking Steps Toward the Goal." In A. Greenwood (ed.), *The National Assessment of College Student Learning: Identification of the Skills to Be Taught, Learned, and Assessed.* Washington, DC: Government Printing Office.

McMillan, J. H. (1987). "Enhancing College Students' Critical Thinking: A Review of Studies." *Research in Higher Education,* 26, 3–29.

Perkins, D., Jay, E., and Tishman, S. (1994). "Assessing Thinking: A Framework for Measuring Critical-Thinking and Problem-Solving Skills at the College Level." In A. Greenwood (ed.), *The National Assessment of College Student Learning: Identification of the Skills to Be Taught, Learned, and Assessed.* Washington, DC: Government Printing Office.

The Watson-Glaser Critical Thinking Appraisal

The Watson-Glaser Critical Thinking Appraisal (CTA) represents an archetype for standardized measures of critical thinking, and it has been used extensively to evaluate the effectiveness of curricula designed to improve critical thinking. Research has found high levels of internal consistency in CTA scores. However, critics have raised questions about the content validity of the CTA and its sensitivity to educational effects. From Assessment Update 8:4 (1996).

As I noted in my last Assessment Measures column, this and the next several columns will focus on various measures of critical thinking. Here I examine the Watson-Glaser Critical Thinking Appraisal (CTA) because it represents an archetype of standardized objective tests of critical thinking ability. Others include the critical thinking subtest of the Collegiate Assessment of Academic Proficiency and the California Critical Thinking Test (see Terenzini and others, 1996). Indeed, researchers have found that correlations between the CTA and other standardized critical thinking tests are quite high (Terenzini and others, 1996).

The CTA is an objective measure of an individual's critical thinking ability that has been used extensively to assess the effectiveness of curricula designed to foster critical thinking (see Crites, 1965; Helmstadter, 1965). The 1964 version of the CTA has two forms, YM and ZM, Both forms of the test, which each take approximately 50 minutes to complete, can be administered in either group or individual settings. In addition to a total score, the CTA provides five subscores: *inference*, the ability to distinguish between true and false inferences made from data; *recognition of assumptions*, the ability to identify unstated assumptions in arguments or assertions; *deduction*, the ability to reason deductively and identify relationships among the elements of a deductive argument; *interpretation*, the ability to weigh evidence and distinguish between generalizations that are warranted by the data and those that are not; and *evaluation of arguments*, the ability to distinguish between arguments that are strong or weak and arguments that are relevant or irrelevant.

Research on the reliability of the CTA has found that the internal consistency of total scores is quite acceptable, ranging from the lower to the upper .80s. Reliability estimates for the CTA subscales are somewhat lower, and users should examine carefully the internal consistency of subscores before using them in assessing program effectiveness. Questions have also been raised about whether the CTA is sufficiently difficult for use with college students (see Crites, 1965; Helmstadter, 1965).

Research on the validity of the CTA has focused on its content, factor structure, and relationship to other measures. Many of the most critical reviews of the CTA have focused on the content of the test, Broadhurst (1970), for example, asked college students to conduct an item analysis of the CTA. On the basis of students' evaluations of the items in the test, he concluded that the CTA is not a valid measure of critical thinking ability. In all fairness, however, the content validity of a test of critical thinking depends on how one defines critical thinking. If one is comfortable with a definition of critical thinking that focuses on the ability to evaluate inferences and assumptions, make deductions, and evaluate argument and interpretation, then the CTA has high content validity. If one has a different definition of critical thinking, then the content validity of the CTA is lower.

Analyses of the structure of the CTA have tended to parallel results I have found for many of the popular tests of general education outcomes. That is, factor analysis results clearly indicate the presence of a dominant general factor, but test items do not load on factors that are consistent with the test developers' a priori scales and subscales (see Follman, Miller, and Burg, 1971). This finding, coupled with relatively low reliability estimates for the subscores, suggests that assessment professionals should exercise caution in their use and interpretation of the CTA subscores.

Several studies have also examined the correlations between CTA scores and other measures in an effort to establish the convergent and discriminant validity of the test. In general, research has found that scores on the CTA are moderately correlated with verbal scores on intelligence tests such as the Weschler Adult Intelligence Scale. These findings led Westbrook and Sellers (1967) to conclude that the CTA measures critical thinking abilities that are not measured by the verbal components of intelligence tests. While some studies have shown that scores on the CTA are higher for students who have participated in specialized critical thinking courses in college (for example, Wilson and Wagner, 1981), other studies have shown that CTA scores are relatively insensitive to college courses that are intended to enhance critical thinking (see Baird, 1988). Based on his review of the literature, Baird cautioned researchers that the CTA may measure a relatively stable construct and as a result the test may be insensitive to educational effects.

Helmstadter's (1965, p. 256) conclusion seems as true today as 30 years ago; "The Watson-Glaser Critical Thinking Appraisal represents a highly professional attempt to measure an important characteristic. And, while there may be some flaws in the test, it is doubtful whether a significantly better measure will be found until there is a major breakthrough either in test technology or in our understanding of the 'thinking' process."

References

Baird, L, L. (1988). "Diverse and Subtle Arts: Assessing the Generic Outcomes of Higher Education." In C. Adleman (ed.), *Performance and Judgment: Essays on Principles and Practice in the Assessment of College Student Learning.* Washington, DC: Government Printing Office.

Broadhurst, N. A. (1970). "An Item Analysis of the Watson-Glaser Critical Thinking Appraisal." *Science Education, 54,* 127–132.

Crites, J. O. (1965). "Test Reviews; Watson-Glaser Critical Thinking Appraisal." *Journal of Counseling Psychology, 12,* 328–331.

Follman, J., Miller, W., and Burg, I. (1971). "Statistical Analysis of Three Critical Thinking Tests." *Educational and Psychological Measurement, 31,* 519–520.

Helmstad ter, G. C. (1965). "Watson-Glaser Critical Thinking Appraisal." *Journal of Educational Measurement, 2,* 254–256.

Terenzini, P. T., Springer, L., Yaeger, P., Pascarella, E. T., and Nora, A. (1996). "First-Generation College Students: Characteristics, Experiences, and Cognitive Development," *Research in Higher Education, 37,* 1–22.

Westbrook, B. W., and Sellers, J. R. (1967). "Critical Thinking, Intelligence, and Vocabulary." *Educational and Psychological Measurement, 27,* 443–446.

Wilson. D. G., and Wagner, E. E. (1981). "The Watson-Glaser Critical Thinking Appraisal as a Predictor of Performance in a Critical Thinking Course." *Educational and Psychological Measurement, 41,* 1319–1322.

The California Critical Thinking Skills Test

The California Critical Thinking Skills Test (CCTST) is a relatively new objective measure of students' critical thinking abilities. Research has found that CCTST scores tend to be higher for students who participate in courses designed to enhance critical thinking skills; however, verbal ability may confound test results. In addition, institutions should carefully evaluate the reliability (i.e., internal consistency) of CCTST scores for their student populations. From Assessment Update *9:2 (1997).*

Developed by Peter Facione, the California Critical Thinking Skills Test (CCTST) is one of several recently developed objective measures of students' critical thinking abilities. It grew out of a two-year Delphi research project sponsored by the American Philosophical Association. The expert panel for the Delphi process included 46 individuals who were actively engaged in critical thinking assessment, education, and research. The report on the panel's work focused on generic critical thinking skills appropriate for first-year students and sophomores completing their general education programs.

The original form of CCTST (Form A) consists of 34 items representing five skills identified by the American Philosophical Association's Delphi process: interpretation, analysis, evaluation, inference, and explanation. A sixth critical thinking skill identified by the panel, metacognition, is not measured by the test. Form B of CCTST was developed by rewriting 28 of the 34 items on Form A. Changes in Form B include differences in names, concepts, and contexts; the types of problems and specific critical thinking skills being assessed were not changed.

The 34 items on both forms of CCTST provide a total score and three subscores: analysis, evaluation, and inference, while 30 items can be used to calculate subscores for inductive and deductive reasoning. In his first technical report, Facione (1990a) noted that the KR20 reliability estimates for the total score ranged from 0.68 to 0.69. Jacobs (1995) reported that alpha reliabilities for Forms A and B were 0.56 and 0.59, respectively. Using the

Spearman-Brown reliability formula to estimate the internal consistency of subtests composed of 34 items, Jacobs found that reliability estimates ranged from 0.14 for analysis to 0.68 for deductive reasoning on Form A and from 0.42 for analysis to 0.71 for deductive reasoning on Form B.

Jacobs (1995) reported that the item means and patterns of item intercorrelations for the two forms were significantly different. However, these differences may have been the result of differences in test takers. Although students were randomly assigned to test forms, it is not possible to say whether item differences were the product of nonequivalent groups or differences in test forms.

In a series of technical reports, Facione (1990b, 1990c) investigated the convergent and discriminant validity of Form A. In his first study, he found that students enrolled in courses designed to enhance critical thinking skills showed significant improvement in their CCTST performance, while students enrolled in courses not so designed did not. Average total scores for students ranged from 15.4 to 16.1 on the pretest, and from 15.5 to 17.4 on the posttest. The 95% confidence interval for groups showing significant gains on CCTST ranged from 1 to 2 points. Given a standard deviation of approximately 4.5 points, the effect sizes for the lower and upper bounds of significant changes ranged from 0.22 to 0.44 standard deviation units.

In subsequent studies, Facione reported that pre- and posttest scores on CCTST were significantly correlated with college grade point average, Scholastic Achievement Test (SAT) verbal and quantitative scores, Nelson-Denny Reading Test scores and English and mathematics placement test scores. CCTST pretest and posttest scores were both significantly correlated with the number of English courses taken in high school, and pretest scores were also significantly correlated with the number of high school mathematics courses taken. In his research Facione found that CCTST scores were significantly related to reading ability as measured by the Nelson-Denny Reading Test. It is not surprising that native speakers of English scored significantly higher than non-native English speakers. Consistent with Facione's research, Jacobs (1995) found that total scores and subscores on Forms A and B were significantly related to SAT verbal and quantitative scores, with the strongest relationships found between CCTST and SAT verbal scores.

Although gender and academic major were not significantly related to students' pretest scores, Facione found that both were related to post-test scores. Specifically, males tended to score higher than females, while students majoring in English, the humanities (excluding the performing arts), mathematics, and engineering scored much higher than students in business and in the performing arts. Students in English, the humanities, mathematics, and engineering also scored higher than students in the natural and social sciences.

Differences in CCTST performance are also related to instructor characteristics. Specifically, number of years of college teaching experience and number of sections of critical thinking courses taught in the prior three years were positively related to CCTST scores. Tenured versus nontenured status, full-time versus part-time employment status, doctoral versus nondoctoral degree, and instructor's gender were not related to CCTST performance. To the extent that teaching effectiveness is related to teaching experience, these findings suggest that performance on the CCTST can be enhanced by the quality of instruction as well as coursework itself.

In sum, CCTST does seem to be sensitive to the educational effects of coursework specifically designed to enhance the critical thinking skills around which the test was designed. However, several questions about the test remain to be answered. These questions center around the psychometric characteristics of Forms A and B, and the influences of reading ability and general verbal ability on test scores. CCTST users would be well advised to examine carefully the reliabilities and item correlations of total scores and subscores for their student populations. Some scores may not have sufficient internal consistency to provide reliable measures of critical thinking at a given institution.

Users should also examine carefully the relationships between entering verbal ability and CCTST scores in order to determine whether changes in test performance represent college effects of uniform change in a stable construct, such as reading or general verbal ability. Even though instructor effects tend to indicate that gains on CCTST are related to quality of instruction, institutions should collect data on both coursework and instruction to distinguish between the two effects. This is particularly important when the goal of assessment is to evaluate the quality of an educational program.

References

Facione, P. A. (1990a). *The California Critical Thinking Skills Test-College Level Technical Report 1: Experimental Validation and Content Validity*. Millbrae: California Academic Press. (ED 015818)

Facione, P. A. (1990b). *The California Critical Thinking Skills Test-College Level Technical Report 2: Factors Predictive of Critical Thinking Skills*. Millbrae: California Academic Press. (ED 015819)

Facione, P. A. (1990c). *The California Critical Thinking Skills Test-College Level Technical Report 3: Gender, Ethnicity, Major, Critical Thinking Self-Esteem, and the CCTST*. Millbrae: California Academic Press. (ED 015962)

Jacobs, S. S. (1995). "Technical Characteristics and Some Correlates of the California Critical Thinking Skills Test Forms A and B." *Research in Higher Education, 36*, 89–108.

Tasks in Critical Thinking

The Tasks in Critical Thinking examination differs from the Watson-Glaser Critical Thinking Appraisal and the California Critical Thinking Skills Test in that it is a constructed-response measure that only provides scores for groups of students. Research suggests that acceptable levels of inter-rater agreement can be achieved when institutions carefully follow the scoring procedures and rubrics provided by the test developer. From Assessment Update 11:6 (1999).

During the past three years I have written several articles reviewing measures of students' critical thinking abilities. My interest stems from a belief that critical thinking is one of the most important outcomes of a college education; at the same time, I recognize that its assessment can be extremely difficult.

One of the recent additions to the arsenal of critical thinking measures is *Tasks in Critical Thinking*, jointly developed by the Educational Testing Service (ETS) and the College Board for the New Jersey Department of Higher Education. Committees of faculty members from New Jersey's two- and four-year colleges and universities worked with ETS to develop *Tasks* as part of the College Outcomes Evaluation Project. These committees also developed the scoring rubrics for *Tasks* and employed the rubrics to evaluate students' responses to assessment conducted throughout the state.

Tasks in Critical Thinking differs from other assessments of critical thinking in two important respects. First, the instrument is a constructed-response or performance measure rather than the typical multiple choice, or recognition, measure seen in most critical thinking assessments. Second, *Tasks* provides a group score rather than individual scores. In its brochure introducing *Tasks*, ETS emphasizes that "the Tasks were not designed for and should not be used to make decisions about individual students. They are intended to provide information about the critical thinking skills of groups of students."

As the name implies, *Tasks in Critical Thinking* sets a task for a student. Specifically, a student must solve a problem by carrying out a series of specific steps. The steps in the assessment are intended to resemble what students are required to do in a class. Each of the problems is set within a specific context or academic area. The three contexts covered by *Tasks* are the humanities, the social sciences, and the natural sciences. Each context area includes three tasks: "Icarus," "The Mystery of the Indo-Europeans," and "Cubism: Cezanne, Picasso, Mondrian" for the humanities; "Facts," "Conland and Teresia," and "Women's Lives" for the social sciences; and "UFOs," "Correlations," and "Lemon Sharks" for the natural sciences.

Although they are context-specific, the problems are designed to be independent of course work. Students are asked to complete a single task or problem. Each of the tasks takes approximately ninety minutes to complete and they are packaged so as to be randomly distributed to students.

Although the measure is named *Tasks in Critical Thinking*, scoring focuses on the skills demonstrated by students in completing the tasks. Students must demonstrate at least two, and often three, skills. The skill areas measured by *Tasks* are inquiry, analysis, and communication. The subskills contained within inquiry include planning a search, using several different methods of observation and discovery, comprehending and extracting information, and sorting and evaluating information. When analysis is the skill being assessed, students may be required to formulate hypotheses and analytical strategies, to apply different techniques or models to solve a problem, to demonstrate flexibility and creativity, to evaluate assumptions or reasoning, and to find relationships or draw conclusions. Subskills included within the communication skill are organizing a presentation, writing effectively, and communicating quantitative or visual information.

Separate scores are provided for each skill being measured by a task. For example, the UFO task might include scores for both inquiry and analysis. Group scores are presented as the percentage of the group demonstrating a particular level of proficiency in a skill area. *Core scoring* is the method used to score *Tasks*; it was developed by ETS for use in performance-based assessment. The score scale for each skill ranges from 1 to 6, with 4 being the core score. The core score is a minimum satisfactory solution for a given problem. Scores of 5 or 6 are awarded only if the core solution is present and the student expands on that solution. Scores of 2 or 3 may be given for partial responses, for minimal development of an idea, or for not providing support for a position. A score of 1 indicates that a student did not demonstrate any level of proficiency in attempting to complete a task. Each task has a scoring rubric that identifies the subskills being measured, the appropriate score levels for each of the subskills, and examples of responses characteristic of each score level.

In the brochure describing *Tasks in Critical Thinking*, ETS notes that at least one hundred students are required for testing. When one hundred students are tested, at least ten students are assigned to each task.

This helps to ensure adequate coverage of skills and subskills and enhances the reliability of group scores. ETS notes that if separate scores are to be reported for subgroups (such as for females and males or for business and education majors) there must be at least one hundred students in each subgroup.

Although assessments that rely on constructed-response formats generally produce lower-reliability coefficients than traditional multiple choice or recognition measures, experience with *Tasks* indicates that acceptable levels of agreement can be achieved when scoring procedures carefully follow the scoring rubrics developed by ETS. The *Core Scoring Manual* provides detailed instructions for planning and conducting local scoring sessions. Other scoring options include local scoring with an ETS consultant and scoring by ETS. Additional information about the effective use of *Tasks* is presented in Peter Ewell's book *A Policy Guide for Assessment: Making Good Use of the Tasks in Critical Thinking*. This book is available from ETS.

The Reflective Judgment Interview

The Reflective Judgment Interview (RJI) is based on a stage model of intellectual development. The interview protocol requires students to consider multiple solutions to a problem, produce a rationale supporting a particular solution, and then evaluate the rationale for that solution. RJI scores have been found to increase with age and years in school, but questions remain about the sensitivity of the measure to specific educational interventions. From Assessment Update 8:5 (1996).

My previous Assessment Measures column profiled the Watson-Glaser Critical Thinking Appraisal. Here I describe an instrument from the opposite end of the measurement spectrum, the Reflective Judgment Interview (RJI) (Kitchener and King, 1981). Despite the fact that the RJI is an extremely labor-intensive measure, Wood (1995) has identified more than 30 studies that have made use of the RJI in research on students' intellectual development and critical thinking.

The RJI is based on a model of intellectual development that describes students' abilities to (1) attend to multiple perspectives or problem solutions, (2) produce defensible rationales in support of multiple solutions, and (3) evaluate the various rationales for problem solutions. These three abilities are represented by seven stages of reflective judgment.

At the first stage of reflective judgment, knowledge is assumed to be absolute and concrete, and knowledge is "knowable" based only on direct observation. At the second level, knowledge is still assumed to be absolute and concrete. However, this knowledge can be based on statements of authorities as well as direct observation. At the third level, knowledge is assumed to be absolute, but it may not be immediately available. Consequently, personal beliefs are seen as a valid source of knowledge. At stage four, knowledge is uncertain, and the rationales for the knowledge arc based on evidence and reason. Knowledge is uncertain at stage five as well. Moreover, evidence and reason are recognized as context-specific. The quality of evidence in support of knowledge claims is also evaluated as strong-weak, relevant-irrelevant, etc. Individuals at the sixth stage view knowledge as constructed from individuals' perspectives, and interpretations can be evaluated by comparing evidence and opinion from multiple perspectives. The seventh and highest level in the reflective judgment hierarchy views judgments as the outcomes of processes of inquiry. Explanatory value, risks of incorrect interpretations, and consequences of alternative judgments are criteria used to evaluate judgments and conclusions.

The RJI consists of a series of brief, complex issues and dilemmas that represent ill-structured problems dealing with ongoing controversies. Typical issues and dilemmas include evolution versus creation, benefits versus dangers of food additives, and the origin of the pyramids. Students are presented an issue or dilemma and then asked to explain their positions via a series of structured probe questions. These questions are asked by a trained and certified interviewer. Students' responses are transcribed and evaluated by two trained raters using a complex, three-digit scoring system. Details of administration and scoring procedures are presented in greater detail by Kitchener and King (1981, 1985) and more recently by King and Kitchener (1994).

Based on his review of studies using the RJI, Wood (1995) reported that median interrater agreement (within dilemmas) is 77%. Forty percent of the studies reported interrater agreement rates greater than 85%, and one-fourth of the studies reported interrater agreement rates in excess of 90%. King and Kitchener (1994) noted that three of the four studies with inter-rater agreement rates below 70% used samples of older adult learners and adult nonstudents. King and Kitchener also reported that the median alpha reliability (across dilemmas) of RJI scores is .85 and ranges from .50 to .96.

Because the RJI is based on a developmental stage model, it is criti-cal that the seven levels in the RJI scoring scheme represent sequential stages of development. Based on his reanalysis of the actual data from studies using the RJI, Wood (1995, p. 43) concluded that "the results of the sequentiality analyses show that the Reflective Judgment Inter-view and scoring system documents a complex developmental sequence. Nonsequential responses are quite rare." King and Kitchener (1994) also reported that growth in reflective judgment (that is, movement through stages) is gradual and not due to test-retest effects.

Performance on the RJI appears to be strongly related to the educa-tional attainment of the students being tested. Wood (1995) reported that samples of students in the early stages of their undergraduate careers tend to score about 3.5 on the RJI, while upperclass undergraduates score at level 4. Beginning graduate students tend to score at about 4.5, and advanced doctoral students tend to score at about a 5.5 level.

In his conclusions, Wood (1995) noted that in his research he found that reflective judgment scores tend to be higher for students from small, selective institutions, although these differences may be due to the en-tering ability of the students (that is, selectivity) rather than institu-tional size. Wood also noted that patterns of RJI scores differ by level of educational attainment. Specifically, the effect of area of study on RJI scores is more pronounced with graduate student samples than with undergraduate samples.

Results to date strongly indicate that use of the RJI to measure student abilities in relation to ill-structured problems generally produces reliable and valid results. However, some caveats are worth mentioning. First, while the RJI produces highly reliable scores with traditional-age students, questions remain about the reliability of the measure when samples include older adult learners and nonstudent adults. Second, the strong relationship of RJI scores to level of educational attainment raises questions about how sensitive the instrument is to specific educational interventions. Finally, additional research is needed on the effects of expertise and field of study on the variability of student performance on the RJI, particularly at higher levels of educational attainment.

References

King, P. M., and Kitchener, K. S. (1994). *Developing Reflective Judgment: Understanding and Promoting Intellectual Growth and Critical Thinking in Adolescents and Adults.* San Francisco: Jossey-Bass.

Kitchener, K. S., and King, P. M. (1981). "Reflective Judgment: Concepts of Justification and Their Relationship to Age and Education." *Journal of Applied Developmental Psychology, 2,* 89–116.

Kitchener, K. S., and King, P. M. (1985). *Reflective Judgment Scoring Manual.*

Wood, P. K. (1995). *A Secondary Analysis of Claims Regarding the Reflective Judgment Interview: Internal Consistency, Sequentiality and Intra-Individual Differences in Ill-Structured Problem Solving.* Columbia: Department of Psychology, University of Missouri.

The CRESST Problem-Solving Measures

Unlike other measures of critical thinking, the CRESST Problem-Solving measure is based on the presumption that critical thinking requires domain-specific knowledge and that the nature of critical thinking differs across disciplines. The CRESST instrument uses knowledge maps to measure content knowledge, short-answer questions to measure problem solving, and self-reports to measure motivation. Re-

search on the psychometric properties of the instrument is limited. However, findings generally support the belief that content-specific knowledge improves critical thinking and problem solving. From Assessment Update *13:4 (2001).*

In six "Assessment Measures" columns in 1996 and 1997, I profiled many of the available measures of students' critical thinking and problem-solving abilities (see *Assessment Update,* vol. 8, nos. 2, 4, and 5; vol. 9, nos. 2, 3, and 6). A criticism of many of the traditional measures of critical thinking and problem solving is that the scores on these measures are strongly related to students' entering ability levels. As a consequence, scores on the Watson-Glaser Critical Thinking Appraisal, the Cornell Critical Thinking Test, and the California Critical Thinking Skills Test show relatively little change after students have participated in programs designed to improve their critical thinking abilities.

Although several qualitative measures of critical thinking, such as the Reflective Judgment Interview, show greater sensitivity to students' college experiences, these measures are difficult and expensive to administer on a large scale. Recently, Phillip Wood and his colleagues at the University of Missouri developed the Reasoning about Current Issues Test (RCIT) as an alternative to both paper-and-pencil and qualitative measures of critical thinking. Preliminary results indicate that scores on the RCIT are moderately sensitive to students' educational experiences, even after controlling for the effects of entering ability. However, scores on the RCIT are also related to level of educational attainment, suggesting that the test may be sensitive to student maturation as well as educational experiences.

A New Approach to Measuring Critical Thinking

Viewing critical thinking as a set of abilities separate from domain-specific knowledge may be the root cause of current critical thinking measures' insensitivity to educational effects. Thus, researchers at the National Center for Research on Evaluation, Standards, and Student

Testing (CRESST) have taken a different approach to the measurement of critical thinking and problem solving based on the belief that "to be a successful problem solver, one must know something (content knowledge), possess intellectual tricks (problem-solving strategies), be able to plan and monitor one's progress toward solving the problem (metacognition), and be motivated to perform (effort and self-efficacy)" (Herl and others, 1999, p. iii). Using this model, CRESST staff have developed a measurement system that includes knowledge maps to measure content knowledge, short-answer questions to measure problem-solving strategies, and self-report questions to measure metacognition and motivation.

Knowledge maps, also termed *concept maps,* comprise *nodes* and *links* (see Herl, Baker, and Niemi, 1996). In a knowledge map, the nodes represent concepts or components in a system, and the links represent the relationships between the concepts or components. For example, one of the knowledge areas assessed in pilot versions of the problem-solving measures dealt with the functioning of a bicycle tire pump. Six main components of a tire pump were identified: cylinder, handle, hose, inlet valve, outlet valve, and piston. Students were instructed to identify the relationships among the six components as causal, contributory, or occurring prior to another component. For example, the handle being up on a tire pump *causes* the pump's piston to be up as well, and an open outlet valve *contributes* to airflow through the hose. (For a detailed description of the knowledge maps used in the problem-solving measures, see Herl and others, 1999.)

Problem-solving strategies are assessed by having students respond with a list to a prompt about problem solving or troubleshooting. In the case of the tire pump, the prompt was "Imagine that the tire pump does not pump air to the hose. What could be wrong?" Students were given two and a half minutes to list all possible reasons for the problem, and their answers were scored against a list of correct answers.

Self-regulation (that is, metacognition and motivation) is measured using 32 self-report items representing four scales: planning, self-monitoring, effort, and self-efficacy. Each scale contains eight items. Scores on the planning and self-monitoring scales are combined to provide a measure of metacognition, and the effort and self-efficacy scores are combined to provide a measure of motivation.

Reliability and Validity Results

Herl and his associates (1999) conducted a series of studies designed to evaluate the reliability and validity of the problem-solving measures. The studies included samples of Taiwanese high school students and undergraduates attending a university in southern California. The studies focused on three issues: (1) reliability and generalizability of the knowledge-mapping and problem-solving strategy scores, (2) structural validity of all three problem-solving measures, and (3) effects of prior domain-specific knowledge on the knowledge-mapping scores. Research focusing on the final issue was intended to evaluate the central assumption of the problem-solving measures, that domain-specific knowledge is a key element in effective problem solving. To test this assumption, a subsample of students was given a diagram of a tire pump and the human respiratory system prior to completing knowledge maps of the two systems. A second group of students was not provided with diagrams in advance.

Analysis of students' scores on the knowledge maps produced generalizability coefficients of 0.65 for U.S. students and 0.34 for Taiwanese students. Presumably, the lower generalizability coefficient for Taiwanese students was due to language difficulties.

Because the scoring of students' problem-solving strategies involved two raters, measures of interrater agreement were calculated. Interrater agreement ranged from 0.62 to 0.86 across subsamples and prompts. Alpha reliability coefficients for the strategy scores ranged from 0.58 to 0.73 for students with prior knowledge and from 0.36 to 0.53 for students who were not given a diagram. The researchers suggest that lack of prior knowledge about a problem may make student performance on the measure less reliable. The generalizability coefficient for the problem-solving strategies measure was 0.66.

Confirmatory factor analysis was used to evaluate the structural validity of the problem-solving measures. Students' knowledge-mapping and strategy scores on the various prompts, as well as the four subscores from the metacognition and motivation questionnaire, were analyzed. Results indicated that a three-factor structure, corresponding to the three parts of the assessment, provided the most appropriate representation of the observed data. The researchers also found that the interfactor correlations were quite low, indicating that problem-solving abilities were represented best by three separate scores rather than a single score.

In the final phase of the validity study, researchers compared the scores of students with prior knowledge (those who were provided with diagrams) to the scores of students who did not have prior knowledge (those who were not provided with diagrams). Results indicated that students who were given diagrams had significantly higher scores on the knowledge-mapping and problem-solving exercises than students who were not given diagrams. Students who were told about the scoring procedures for the knowledge-mapping exercises did not score significantly higher than other students, and there were no significant differences between the scores of males and females. These findings led the researchers to conclude that prior domain-specific knowledge does have a positive effect on problem solving.

Overall, the results of this study led Herl and his colleagues to conclude that the CRESST problem-solving measures can provide reliable and valid information about students' problem-solving abilities at the group level. The relatively low generalizability coefficients for individuals led them to conclude that the measures should not be used to assess individual students. From my perspective, the most significant lesson to be learned from this research is not that a new measure of critical thinking may soon be available. Rather, this project demonstrates that precisely defining what is to be measured, and then carefully crafting instruments that measure all of the specifications of the domain, offers the greatest promise for collecting assessment data that accurately represent important aspects of student learning and development.

References

Herl, H. E., Baker, E. L., and Niemi, D. (1996). "Construct Validation of an Approach to Modeling the Cognitive Structure of U.S. History Knowledge." *Journal of Educational Research*, 89, 206–219.

Herl, H. E., O'Neil, H. F., Jr., Chung, G.K.W.K., Bianchi, C., Wang, S., Mayer, R., Lee, C. Y., Choi, A., Suen, T., and Tu, A. (Mar. 1999). *Final Report for Validation of Problem-Solving Measures*. Technical Report 501. Los Angeles: Center for the Study of Evaluation, University of California.

Value-Added Assessment

Freshman-to-Senior Gains at the University of Tennessee, Knoxville

In 1989, researchers at the University of Tennessee, Knoxville (UTK) began a longitudinal study of student gains in learning. Almost 1,000 students completed the COMP Objective Test as freshmen and as seniors. Results failed to identify meaningful relationships between students' curricular and co-curricular experiences and their score gains on the COMP exam. Instead, score gains were significantly and negatively related to initial academic aptitude. From Assessment Update 4:2 (1992).

In one state—Tennessee—the higher education commission bases a percentage of the annual allocation of public funds for higher education instruction on institutional mean scores, mean score gain, and efforts taken to improve students' scores on the ACT-COMP exam. For most institutions in Tennessee, awards for score gain are based on "estimated" gain scores (see my column in the January–February 1992 issue). In 1987, researchers at the University of Tennessee, Knoxville, published an article questioning the validity of using estimated score gain on the COMP exam as an indicator of general education program effectiveness (Banta and others, 1987). The UTK researchers concluded: "No institution can have a clear idea of the amount of student growth its general education program may be promoting until it tests its own incoming students, then administers an equivalent form of the same test to graduates" (p. 216).

As a result of the 1987 findings, a comprehensive study of student growth in college, as measured by actual freshman-to-senior gain scores on the COMP exam, was undertaken at the University of Tennessee, Knoxville, in 1989. The subjects were 942 seniors who had taken the COMP Objective Test first as freshmen, then as seniors. Sources of data included the following: (1) ACT Assessment composite scores, college grades, and transcripts showing courses taken in college, obtained from student records for 873 of the students having freshman and senior COMP scores; (2) responses to the senior survey (designed to gather information about faculty-student interaction, peer interaction, and attendance at campus cultural events), obtained for 722 of the double-tested seniors; and (3) the College Student Experiences Questionnaire (CSEQ), administered to 120 paid volunteers from the double-tested senior sample.

The analysis of freshman-to-senior gains was accomplished in three phases: (1) profiles of students with the highest gain scores (upper quartile) and lowest gain scores (bottom quartile) were compared; (2) an exploration of the relationships between college experiences, as measured by the UTK Senior Survey and the CSEQ, was undertaken; and (3) an evaluation of the relationship between coursework (obtained from student transcripts) and gain scores was undertaken.

Analysis of high and low gain groups indicated that seniors with the highest gain scores differed most from those with the lowest gain scores in aptitude and achievement. Those with *highest gains* had *lower* ACT Assessment composite scores, ACT English and mathematics scores, and cumulative grade point averages than did seniors with low gain scores. The group with high gain also had lower COMP total scores and subscores as freshmen. The high and low gain groups did not differ on any of the CSEQ quality of effort or involvement scales, nor on any of the scales from the Senior Survey. In terms of coursework, students with low gain scores took fewer business courses and more natural science courses. (Regarding this last finding, it is worth noting that the relationships between coursework and gain were extremely weak.)

Canonical variate analysis was used to explore the relationship between involvement in the college experience (CSEQ and Senior Survey scales) and COMP gain. Data from the CSEQ indicated that investing effort in library experience and experience with faculty produced gains in the categories Using the Arts and Communicating, but spending time in clubs and organizations and in writing activities retarded growth in those categories. Analysis of the Senior Survey responses revealed more contradictory evidence: interacting with peers and attending campus events fostered growth in the category Clarifying Values, but inhibited gains in Communicating. Canonical redundancy analysis further indicated that the quality of effort measures of the CSEQ explained only 5% of the variance in subscore gain, while less than 1% of the variance in subscore gain was accounted for by scales from the senior survey.

Three approaches were used to assess the impact of coursework on gain scores. First, cluster analysis was employed to identify groups of courses that *maximized* score gain on one or more COMP subscales. Four coursework clusters were identified. In general, above-average gains on one COMP subscale were offset by below-average gains on another. Thus, differences in coursework had virtually no effect on gain in total score.

In the second set of analyses concerning coursework and gain, a three-step process was employed to investigate the relationships between actual patterns of course taking and gain scores. Multivariate analysis of covariance did not identify a significant effect on COMP gain of coursework actually taken.

In the final set of analyses, data on actual patterns of coursework and gain scores were again evaluated using a latent variable model of change. This analysis confirmed that actual course-taking patterns at UTK had no significant effect on student growth as measured by COMP gain (Pike, 1991).

In summary, the analysis of freshman-to-senior gains produced a number of disturbing findings. The first was the absence of any meaningful relationship between students' investment of time and effort and score gain on the COMP exam. The absence of clear relationships between score gain and college coursework was a second disturbing finding. The significant *negative* relationship between gain and initial (freshman) academic aptitude was perhaps the most disturbing result of the freshman-to-senior gains study because it suggested that the most effective method of improving student score gain on the COMP exam is for an institution to attract less well prepared students.

In the freshman-to-senior gains study, and in my research (Pike, in press), the UTK researchers examined possible reasons for their counterintuitive findings. They concluded that gain scores are probably not valid measures of student learning and development. The reliability estimate for individual gain scores was found to be unacceptably low (.14) and the 95% confidence interval for mean gain scores was well over 20 points. The UTK researchers also concluded that the negative correlation between gain and freshman COMP scores was probably a spurious relationship produced by measurement error. Moreover, this spurious relationship was found to be responsible for many of the counterintuitive findings. The researchers concluded, as did Lee Cronbach and Lita Furby (1970, p. 80): "It appears that investigators who ask questions regarding gain scores would ordinarily be better advised to frame their questions in other ways."

References

Banta, T. W., Lambert, E. W., Pike, G. R., Schmidhammer, J. L., and Schneider, J. A. (1987). "Estimated Student Score Gain on the ACT COMP Exam: Valid Tool for Institutional Assessment?" *Research in Higher Education, 27*, 195–217.

Cronbach, L. J., and Furby, L. (1970). "How Should We Measure 'Change'—Or Should We?" *Psychological Bulletin, 74*, 68–80.

Pike, G. R. (1991). "Using Structural Equation Models with Latent Variables to Study Student Growth and Development." *Research in Higher Education, 52*, 499–524.

Pike, G. R. (1992). "Lies, Damn Lies, and Statistics Revisited: A Comparison of Three Methods of Representing Change." *Research in Higher Education, 33*, 71–84.

Methods of Evaluating Student Change During College

There are a variety of measures and statistical techniques that can be used to represent students' intellectual growth and development during college. These approaches include gain scores, estimated gains scores, residual scores, mixed-effect models, and growth curves. Gains scores and estimated gain scores are the easiest method to use, but appear to be the least accurate. Residual scores, mixed-effect models, and growth curves are more demanding technically, but appear to be more appropriate for measuring change during college. From Assessment Update 6:2 (1994).

I must confess that this is not the column I had planned to write. About a week ago, I was contacted by a state higher education commission about the feasibility of developing measures of "value added" for *College BASE*. Although this topic has been the subject of one "Assessment Measures" column and rejoinder and response columns (see *Assessment Update*, 1992, Vol. 4, No. 2), I feel compelled to return to the issue of assessing student change during college. My purpose is to acquaint readers with some of the options available to institutions interested in studying student change and to provide a set of references on the measurement of change.

The rationale for studying student change is convincing. Numerous authors argue that change is a fundamental feature of higher education and must be studied. These individuals also argue that studies of how students change during their college careers provide a more accurate representation of educational effects than do traditional outcomes studies because they eliminate the confounding effects of differences in ability levels. Other often-cited advantages of studying change include encouraging faculty and administrators to think in developmental terms, promoting greater faculty and student involvement in assessment, and providing outcomes measures that are appropriate for nontraditional programs and students.

While there is virtually unanimous agreement that student change during college should be assessed, there is little agreement about *how* it should be assessed. In the remainder of this column, I will review several methods of representing change during college. Readers who hope I will identify the "right" way of studying change will be disappointed; I firmly believe that there is no right way. Furthermore, the method that may be most useful for one campus may not be the most useful method for another campus.

Gain Scores. One of the most widely publicized and used methods of studying change during college is the gain score. Until recently, this was a criterion for awarding state funding supplements in Tennessee. Gain scores are regularly reported by the College Outcome Measures Program (COMP) staff as indicators of student learning and program effectiveness. Calculating a gain score entails administering an instrument to students at the beginning of a program of study and then readministering the instrument on completion of the program. The difference between the two scores is a measure of student growth, and the average of all students' scores is a measure of institution, or program, effectiveness. Steele (1989) has provided a detailed discussion of how gain scores can be used for program evaluation.

The articles by Steele and myself in the previous *Assessment Update* provide an indication of the controversial nature of gain scores. In addition to that discussion, those interested in considering gain scores may wish to consult the articles by Baird (1988), Linn (1981), and Pike (1992a).

Estimated Gain Scores. One limitation of using gain scores is that assessment researchers must wait at least two or four years before they have any data on program outcomes. Partly in response to the long timelines in studies of student gain, the developers of the COMP exam have offered to provide an *estimate* of student gain in total score. Using the fact that the correlation between ACT Assessment composite scores and freshman COMP scores is approximately 0.70, ACT has developed concordance tables that allow an institution to estimate mean freshman COMP scores for a group of graduating students who have valid ACT Assessment scores. The mean estimated freshman score for an institution is then subtracted from the mean score for the same cohort of graduating students to provide an estimate of gain.

The use of estimated score gain in outcomes assessment has been discussed by Steele (1989) and Banta and others (1987). Although estimated gain eliminates the need for longitudinal studies covering several years, institutions should not adopt this method without some careful research. Assessment professionals need to determine that the estimates for freshman scores are appropriate for their campuses. Estimates derived from a national data set may not be appropriate for a specific campus. Further, as an institution adopts a new form of a test, the estimates of freshman scores on that test must be checked to see whether they are still valid. Another potential limitation of the method is that entering ACT Assessment scores may not be available for some graduating students. Banta and others (1987) compared graduating seniors who did and did not have ACT Assessment scores and found that the two groups differed in race, socioeconomic status, high school grade point average, and college experiences.

Residual Scores. In his most recent book, Astin (1993) advocates the use of residual scores in assessing the net effects of college. Residual scores are calculated by regressing students' scores at the end of a program of study on one or more entry measures in order to develop a prediction model. According to Astin, the differences between actual and predicted scores represent the net effects of college experiences. This approach is being used by the National Center on Postsecondary Teaching, Learning and Assessment to study college effects (Pascarella, personal communication). Technical discussions of the strengths and limitations of residual scores can be found in research by Astin (1993), Baird (1988), and Pike (1992a).

An approach related to the use of residual scores, the use of fixed-effect structural equation models to study change, is discussed by Pike (1991). A primary limitation of this method is that it is very demanding technically (statistically).

Mixed-Effect Models. All of the approaches discussed thus far seek to assess student achievement at the end of a program of study after *controlling* for differences in entering achievement (for example, freshman test scores). These approaches represent a general class of statistical analyses that can be termed fixed-effect models. Recently, authors such as Muthén (1991) have suggested approaches based on mixed- or random-effects models. Instead of seeking to eliminate individual differences using statistical procedures, random-effects models explicitly consider individual differences in change. McLean and Sanders at the University of Tennessee, Knoxville, have proposed a method of using mixed models for teacher evaluation that deserves additional study. Readers interested in learning more about that approach should contact the authors directly. The mixed-effects approach advocated by McLean and Sanders makes use of measured variables. Other authors have suggested that mixed-effects models be used with latent (unmeasured) variables to study student change (Knight, 1993; Muthén, 1991; Pike, 1992b).

Growth Curves. If institutions are willing to invest the time and resources to gather data about student learning at more than two points in time, a whole new set of methods for studying student change becomes available. This class of methods involves modeling student growth or learning curves at multiple points in time. Discussions of these approaches are available in the works of Bryk and Raudenbush (1992) and Willett (1988).

As I stated at the outset, assessing how students change during college is an important undertaking, but it is not easy. The difficulty is apparent in the fact that while almost 90% of all colleges and universities are implementing assessment programs, only about 10% to 15% are attempting to study how students change during their college careers. I strongly encourage assessment professionals to examine the various methods available for studying change, to identify methods that might be used by their institution, and then to evaluate carefully the appropriateness of using those methods in their own settings.

References

Astin, A. W. (1993). *What Matters in College?* San Francisco: Jossey-Bass.

Baird, L. L. (1988). "Value-Added: Using Student Gains as Yardsticks of Learning." In C. Adelman (ed.), *Performance and Judgment: Essays on Principles and Practice in the Assessment of College Student Learning* (pp. 205–216). Washington, DC: U.S. Government Printing Office. Document No. OR88-514.

Banta, T. W., Lambert, E. W., Pike, G. R., Schmidhammer, J. L., and Schneider, J. A. (1987). "Estimated Student Score Gain on the ACT COMP Exam: Valid Tool for Institutional Assessment?" *Research in Higher Education, 27*, 195–217.

Bryk, A. S., and Raudenbush, S. W. (1992). *Hierarchical Linear Models: Applications and Data Analysis Methods*. Newbury Park, CA: Sage.

Knight, W. E. (1993). "An Examination of Freshman to Senior General Education Gains Across a National Sample of Institutions with Different General Education Requirements Using a Mixed-Effect Structural Equation Model." *Research in Higher Education, 34*, 41–54.

Linn, R. L. (1981). "Measuring Pretest-Posttest Performance Changes." In R. A. Berk (ed.), *Educational Evaluation Methodology: The State of the Art* (pp. 84–109). Baltimore: Johns Hopkins University Press.

Muthén, B. O. (1991). "Analysis of Longitudinal Data Using Latent Variable Models with Varying Parameters." In L. M. Collins and J. L. Horn (eds.), *Best Methods for the Analysis of Change* (pp. 1–17). Washington, DC: American Psychological Association.

Pike, G. R. (1991). "Using Structural Equation Models with Latent Variables to Study Student Growth and Development." *Research in Higher Education, 32*, 499–524.

Pike, G. R. (1992a). "Lies, Damn Lies, and Statistics Revisited: A Comparison of Three Methods of Representing Change." *Research in Higher Education, 33*, 71–84.

Pike, G. R. (1992b). "Using Mixed-Effect Structural Equation Models to Study Student Academic Development." *Review of Higher Education, 15*, 151–178.

Steele, J. M. (1989). "Evaluating College Programs Using Measures of Student Achievement and Growth." *Educational Evaluation and Policy Analysis, 11*, 357–375.

Willett, J. B. (1988). "Questions and Answers in the Measurement of Change." In E. Rothkopf (ed.), *Review of Research in Education* (pp. 345–422). Washington, DC: American Educational Research Association.

Revisiting the Blind Alley of Value Added

Trudy W. Banta, Gary R. Pike

The value added by a college education continues to be a central concern of government leaders and policy makers. Despite the popularity of the concept, substantial concerns arise about the reliability and validity of the various measures of value added. Several scholars have suggested that measuring change during college may be more appropriate for assessments of disciplinary knowledge than generic skills. From Assessment Update *19:1 (2007).*

The Commission on the Future of Higher Education appointed by Secretary of Education Margaret Spellings issued a report in September 2006 entitled *A Test of Leadership: Charting the Future of U.S. Higher Education* (U.S. Department of Education, 2006). Two key commission recommendations are stated: "Higher education institutions should measure student learning using quality assessment data" and "The results of student learning assessments, including value-added measurements that indicate how much students' skills have improved over time, should be made available to students and reported in the aggregate publicly" (p. 23). Anticipating such recommendations, in its Spring 2006 issue of *Perspectives*, the American Association of State Colleges and Universities issued the following statement in an article entitled "Value-Added Assessment: Accountability's New Frontier": "Value-added assessment allows true comparisons of the difference college makes to students across institutions and institutional types, instead of simply reflecting institutional resources and/or reputation" (p. 3). Interest in measuring what students learn in college and using one or a limited number of standardized instruments (thus permitting institutional comparisons) to do that has probably never been more intense. Our purpose in this article is to raise some questions about the capacity of standardized instruments to measure gain, or value added. We describe the ways in which change or growth and development can be measured and summarize what experts over the past four decades have concluded about the reliability and usability of these approaches.

Research-Based Conclusions About Value Added

In a brief, accessible article in a 1984 issue of the *AAHE Bulletin* entitled "The Blind Alley of Value Added," Jonathan Warren, who had spent a portion of his career at the Educational Testing Service (ETS), summed up the thinking of measurement specialists at that time: "In the abstract, the logic of value added gives it great appeal. In practice, I'll argue, it seldom leads anywhere. Its results are too often trivial, difficult to make sense of, and peripheral to most instructional purposes. An undue focus on value added may mean that today's opportunity to improve quality will slip away from us" (p. 10). "For practical purposes, value added isn't a workable concept and we have to get on with alternative ways of looking at the effect of what we do" (p. 12).

In a careful review of the literature on value-added assessment published in 1988, Leonard Baird, also a measurement expert employed for a time at ETS, concluded, "If executed thoughtfully, value-added assessment has some potential for the improvement of instruction at the program level. It is much less appropriate or useful at the institutional level of analysis. It is, above all, not a panacea, or even a solution to be recommended widely" (p. 215).

For a decade that began in the mid-1980s, we were responsible for testing several thousand freshmen and seniors at the University of Tennessee, Knoxville (UTK) in response to the state's performance funding mandate. In 1992, Gary Pike published the results of an empirical study involving 722 students who had taken the ACT College Outcome Measures Project (COMP) exam, first as freshmen, then again as seniors at UTK. Pike investigated the reliability of gain (value added), using three methods: gain scores, residual scores, and repeated measures. He found that all three methods of representing change had serious shortcomings.

In the early 1990s, measurement specialists apparently believed they had said all that was needed to put the concept of value added in higher education to rest and turned their attention to other topics. In 2005, however, attempts to use student score gain to measure effectiveness of K–12 teachers prompted officials at ETS to commission Henry Braun to write a primer on value-added models. Braun (2005) observed that "the statistical models underlying [value-added measures] were originally developed for use in settings, such as agriculture, in which randomized experiments and sufficient data are the norm. [In these settings,] endowing statistical estimates with causal interpretations is relatively straightforward" (p. 16). But school systems do not operate by assigning students, then teachers, randomly to classes. For this and other reasons, Braun concluded, "reliance on a single statistical measure cannot be recommended" (p. 16). And in his October 2005 letter to individuals receiving a copy of Braun's primer, ETS president and CEO Kurt Landgraf stated, "Results from value-added models should not serve as the primary basis for making consequential decisions. Other measures must be included in any fair and valid teacher evaluation system."

As compelling as the concept of measuring student growth and development in college, or value added, may be, research does not support the use of standardized tests for this purpose.

A Brief Explanation of Value-Added Concerns

There are two basic methods of representing change during college. The first method involves calculating difference scores. If a test is administered at entry and again at graduation, the difference between scores can be used to represent value added. This approach is used in Tennessee as part of the state's performance funding program. The second method of representing value added is to regress exiting scores on entering scores. The difference between the expected score produced by the regression model and the actual score at exit (that is, the residual) can also be used to represent value added. This is a form of analysis of covariance and is the approach employed by the Collegiate Learning Assessment .

Three key questions must be answered about the utility of value-added measures and the confidence we can place in them. Are the measures reliable? Do the measures accurately represent what students have learned? What measure should be used?

Questions about the reliability of difference scores were a focus of early criticisms of value added. Carl Bereiter (1963) and Lee Cronbach and Lita Furby (1970) observed that the reliability of difference scores is extremely low. Moreover, as the correlation between measures at entry and exit increases, the reliability of the difference score decreases. Ross Traub (1967) observed that the reliability of residual scores is also quite low and tends to decrease as the correlation between entry and exit scores increases. Not surprisingly, Pike's study (1992) of ACT comp scores found that the reliability for a difference score was 0.14 and the reliability for a residual score was 0.17—a very poor showing, indeed.

The second question that arises in discussions of value added is whether the measures accurately represent student learning. Scholars such as Robert L. Thorndike (1966) have criticized difference scores because pretest-posttest differences are almost always negatively correlated with entering scores. That is, students with low scores at entry gain more than students with high entering scores. This feature of difference scores is an artifact of floor and ceiling effects for the tests and the fact that the measurement error in entering test scores is included in the difference score, but with the sign reversed. Residual scores also have been criticized for not representing student learning. In fact, Baird (1988) argued that residual scores were not a measure of change. Because regression analysis removes all of the variance in exiting scores that is linearly related to entering scores, residual scores will underestimate student learning if there is any linear relationship between learning and entering ability. Concerns related to the first two questions suggest that value-added analysis will not yield accurate and appropriate information about student learning within institutions.

Last but certainly not least, the decision about which approach to use is not trivial. Frederic Lord (1967, 1969) examined weight gain in males and females during college, using difference scores and analysis of covariance (that is, residual scores). When the analyses used difference scores, Lord found no differences in weight gain for males and females. However, when the same data were analyzed using residual scores, there was a significant difference in weight gain for males and females. Known as "Lord's Paradox," this phenomenon raises serious concerns about the ability to compare institutions or groups within institutions using a value-added standard. In fact, Lord (1967) concluded, "there simply is no logical or statistical procedure that can be counted on to make proper allowances for uncontrolled pre-existing differences between groups" (p. 305).

Alternative Measures

In his 1988 review article, Baird observed, "The more tests assess general characteristics, the less sensitive they are to change due to educational programs. That is, the tests become so general as to assess relatively stable characteristics of students. In the cognitive area, the more general tests border on measures of general intelligence" (pp. 206–207). This statement strongly suggests that testing students' discipline-specific knowledge and skills as well as their generic skills (writing, speaking, critical thinking) as applied in their major fields of study provides a much more promising avenue for assessing growth and development in college than do today's most commonly discussed tests of generic skills alone. We support a focus on major field assessment, with an emphasis on using student electronic portfolios as the most authentic instrument for demonstrating growth over time.

In yet another ETS publication, *A Culture of Evidence: Postsecondary Assessment and Learning Outcomes,* Carol Dwyer, Catherine Millett, and David Payne (2006) also support a discipline-based approach, recommending that "the United States create a system that will assess workforce readiness" (p. 19). They argue that "from an economic perspective [workforce readiness] has direct links to the economic competitiveness of the United States in a global economy" (p. 19). Dwyer, Millett, and Payne observe that professional fields such as education, social work, nursing, law, and medicine already have measures of workforce readiness or domain-specific knowledge sufficient for workforce entry. They suggest that "appropriate academic organizations" (p. 20) in fields currently without such measures be charged "with the task of articulating a set of expected learning outcomes" (p. 20) and a set of pre- and post-measures for assessing growth in those fields.

Conclusion

Given the weight of evidence offered by prominent measurement experts over the past forty years, we must conclude that pursuing the concept of value added condemns us to revisit a blind alley. We offer this very brief review of literature and the lists of references and additional resources that follow in the hope that they will provide colleagues in higher education with some reasoned arguments to use in addressing the current press to assess with a standardized test and to compare institutions by using value-added measures.

References

American Association of State Colleges and Universities. (Spring 2006). "Value-Added Assessment: Accountability's New Frontier." *Perspectives*.

Baird, L. L. (1988). "Value-Added: Using Student Gains as Yardsticks of Learning." In C. Adelman (ed.), *Performance and Judgment: Essays on Principles and Practice in the Assessment of College Student Learning*. Washington, DC: U.S. Government Printing Office.

Bereiter, C. (1963). "Some Persisting Dilemmas in the Measurement of Change." In Harris (ed.), *Problems with Measuring Change*. Madison: University of Wisconsin Press.

Braun, H. I. (2005). *Using Student Progress to Evaluate Teachers: A Primer on Value-Added Models*. Princeton, NJ: Policy Evaluation and Research Center, Educational Testing Service.

Cronbach, L. J., and Furby, L. (1970). "How Should We Measure Change—or Should We?" *Psychological Bulletin, 74*, 68–80.

Dwyer, C. A., Millett, C. M., and Payne, D. G. (2006). *A Culture of Evidence: Postsecondary Assessment and Learning Outcomes*. Princeton, NJ: Educational Testing Service.

Lord, F. M. (1967). "A Paradox in the Interpretation of Group Comparisons." *Psychological Bulletin, 68*, 304–305.

Lord, F. M. (1969). "Statistical Adjustments When Comparing Preexisting Groups." *Psychological Bulletin, 72*, 336–337.

Pike, G. R. (1992). "Lies, Damn Lies, and Statistics Revisited: A Comparison of Three Methods of Representing Change." *Research in Higher Education, 33*, 71–84.

Thorndike, R. L. (1966). "Intellectual Status and Intellectual Growth." *Journal of Educational Psychology, 57*, 121–127.

Traub, R. E. (1967). "A Note on the Reliability of Residual Change Scores." *Journal of Educational Measurement, 4*, 253–256.

U.S. Department of Education. (2006). *A Test of Leadership: Charting the Future of U.S. Higher Education*. Washington, DC: U.S. Department of Education. Also available at [http://www.ed.gov/about/bdscomm/list/hiedfuture/reports /pre-pub-report.pdf].

Warren, J. (1984). "The Blind Alley of Value Added." *AAHE Bulletin, 37*(1), 10–13.

Additional Resources

Hanson, G. R. (1988). "Critical Issues in the Assessment of Value Added in Education." In T. W. Banta (ed.), *Implementing Outcomes Assessment: Promise and Perils*. New Directions for Institutional Research, no. 59. San Francisco: Jossey-Bass.

Harris, C. W. (1963). *Problems in Measuring Change*. Madison: University of Wisconsin Press.

Holland, P. W., and Rubin, D. B. (1983). "On Lord's Paradox." In H. Wainer and S. Messick (eds.), *Principals of Modern Psychological Measurement: A Festschrift for Frederic M. Lord*. Hillsdale, NJ: Erlbaum.

Linn, R. L., and Slinde, J. A. (1977). "The Determination of the Significance of Change Between Pre- and Post-Testing Periods." *Review of Educational Research, 47*, 121–150.

Terenzini, P. T. (1989). "Measuring the Value of College: Prospects and Problems." In C. Fincher (ed.), *Assessing Institutional Effectiveness: Issues, Methods, and Management*. Athens: University of Georgia Press.

Willett, J. B. (1988). "Questions and Answers in the Measurement of Change." In E. Z. Rothkopf (ed.), *Review of Research in Education, 15*, 345–422. Washington, DC: American Educational Research Association.